France and South Africa: towards a new engagement with Africa

FRANCE AND SOUTH AFRICA: TOWARDS A NEW ENGAGEMENT WITH AFRICA

Chris Alden and Guy Martin (editors)

Protea Book House
Pretoria
2003

France and South Africa: towards a new engagement with Africa
Chris Alden and Guy Martin (editors)

First edition, 2003
Protea Book House
PO Box 35110, Menlo Park, 0102
protea@intekom.co.za

Typography and design by Hennie Vermaak
Cover design by Tienie du Plessis
Reproduction by PrePress Images, Pretoria
Printed and bound by Interpak Books, Pietermaritzburg

ISBN 1-86919-002-5

© 2003, Chris Alden and Guy Martin (editors)
© All rights reserved.
No part of this book may be reproduced in any form, without prior permission in writing from the publisher.

ACKNOWLEDGEMENTS

The editors would like to thank the following people and organisations, all of whom in various ways have provided support for this project. The Institute for Global Dialogue, the French Institute of South Africa, the Department of International Relations at the University of the Witwatersrand, the Department of Foreign Affairs in Pretoria, and the French Embassy. In South Africa, Garth le Pere, Kato Lambrechts, Georges Herault, Marie-Odile Blanc, Aziz Pahad, and Roland Dubertrand. Among the contributors, Ali Mazrui and Roger Southall kindly provided their pieces though they were not originally participants to the project. In London, Jennifer Chapa provided able assistance in putting the manuscript together in short order. Finally, Kato Lambrechts deserves special thanks for embarking on a translation 'au dernier instant'.

CONTRIBUTORS

Chris Alden is a lecturer in international relations at the London School of Economics.

Jean-Francois Bayart is the director of the *Centre d'etudes de recherches internationales* (CERI), Paris and an international scholar of African studies.

Daniel Bourmaud is a professor of political science at INALCO-CDNRS, Paris 1 University.

Roland Dubertrand is a diplomat attached to the French Ministry of Foreign Affairs.

Phillipe Hugon is a professor of economics and director of CERED/FORUM, University of Paris X – Nanterre.

Guy Martin is a visiting associate professor in the department of government and foreign affairs, the University of Virginia.

Ali Mazrui is the director of the Institute of Global Cultural Studies and Albert Schweitzer Professor of Humanities at Binghamton University, SUNY and an international scholar of African studies.

Aziz Pahad is the deputy minister in the South African department of foreign affairs.

Roger Southall is a professor of politics at Rhodes University, Grahamstown.

CONTENTS

Introduction: Chris Alden and Guy Martin 9

Part One: France and South Africa in Africa: a historical perspective 11
Chapter 1: "France and Africa: the constant striving for exceptionalism" Daniel Bourmaud (University of Paris 1) 13
Chapter 2: "South Africa in Africa: the apartheid regime's foreign policy in sub-Saharan Africa" Roger Southall (Rhodes University) 31

Part Two: The Africa policies of France and South Africa 73
Chapter 3: "The reform of French policy in Africa: modernising and opening up" Roland Dubertrand (French Ministry of Foreign Affairs) 75
Chapter 4: "South Africa's Africa policy" Aziz Pahad (South African Deputy Minister of Foreign Affairs) . . . 81
Chapter 5: "France's Africa policy in transition: disengagement and redeployment" Guy Martin (University of Virginia) 93
Chapter 6: "The economic relations of France and South Africa with Africa" Philippe Hugon (University of Paris X - Nanterre) 111
Chapter 7: "Between conflict and co-operation: Franco-South African relations in the African context" Chris Alden (London School of Economics) . . . 129

Part Three: France and South Africa: issues and challenges 143
Chapter 8: "The language of the francophonie and the race of the renaissance: a Commonwealth perspective" Ali Mazrui (New York University) 145
Chapter 9: "The war in Africa: a challenge for Paris and Pretoria" Jean-Francois Bayart (CERI Paris) 163

General bibliography 179

INTRODUCTION

Chris Alden & Guy Martin

Any examination of the foreign policies of two states will be punctuated by notions of comparison, of areas of difference and similarity, in the comportment and conduct of policy towards a given sphere. This study of France and South Africa and the changing nature of their relationship with the African continent, without deliberately seeking it out, invites such comparison through the structuring of the various themes addressed in the chapters of this book. There is obviously much more that separates the two states than binds their experience together, be it in the realm of history, the trajectory of economic development or the elaboration of culture. Furthermore, the artificiality of 'proximity', so long a part of the French rationale for its African policy in the aftermath of colonialism, and notional belief in 'separateness', a pillar of white South Africa's domestic and foreign policy towards Africa, were never more than ideological underpinnings for the pursuit of cruder political and economic strategies rooted in racially motivated hegemony. But, these obvious considerations must nonetheless be tempered by the historical fact of French involvement in continental affairs, which has made it the continent's leader in development assistance, by the dominance of French institutions and language in nearly half of the continent, and by influence of Africa over aspects of French politics, society and culture. So too, the patent reality of South Africa's geography cannot serve to deny the particularity of its political, economic and social experience (what the Marxists once characterised as 'colonialism of a special type'), something that today has translated into it exercising an unprecedented and increasing degree of influence over many aspects of continental affairs.

This same problematic history of French and South African interaction with Africa argues for a closer examination of this phenomenon as the two states attempt to shed the atavistic policies of the past and move into a new phase of relations with the continent. In a very genuine sense, the relative decline of traditional French interests in Africa, a product of the shifting agenda of post-Cold War and European politics, has paved the way for a new engagement with Africa shorn of its colonial vestiges. Chastened by past failures, from the Bokassa affair to France's part in the Rwandan tragedy, enlightened French policy makers are grappling with the construction of an approach to the continent that is based upon mutual respect and interests. In the case of South Africa, the collapse of the apartheid regime has given way to a new government committed to the integration of human rights within its foreign policy towards Africa. The idea of an 'African renaissance', a South African reconception of the old pan-Africanist dream, offers a vision of African renewal with South African policy makers, business people, intellectuals and finance playing the part of catalyst. How these changes in policy towards the African continent in both Paris and Pretoria have affected political and economic relations; how these changes are being realised; what the impact of new approaches to Africa means for the continent is the subject of this book.

The first chapter by Daniel Bourmaud introduces the parameters of French policy towards Africa from the final pages of the colonial era to the end of the Cold War. The second chapter, a contribution by Roger Southall, provides a historical overview of South Africa's interaction with the African continent through the same period of time. Roland Dubertrand, the First Counsellor at the French Embassy in Pretoria, presents an insight into his government's Africa policy in the third chapter. In the next chapter Aziz Pahad, South Africa's Deputy Foreign Minister, provides his government's perspective on the challenges facing the post-apartheid government in Africa. In Chapter Five, Guy Martin assesses the changing nature of French policy towards Africa. This is followed by Phillip Hugon's chapter on the economic character of the relationship between France and Africa and South Africa and the rest of the continent since 1990. In Chapter Seven, Chris Alden looks at bi-lateral relations between France and South Africa in the contemporary period. In the following chapter, Ali Mazrui, the eminent African scholar, considers the nature of language and culture in an African Renaissance. Finally, Jean-Francois Bayart, a leading Africanist and theorist of the state, provides a provicative look at the persistence of war in Africa.

PART ONE:
FRANCE AND SOUTH AFRICA IN AFRICA: A HISTORICAL PERSPECTIVE

Chapter One:

FRANCE AND AFRICA: THE CONSTANT STRIVING FOR EXCEPTIONALISM

Daniel Bourmaud

France's policy in Africa has never ceased to intrigue. The drastic changes which swept through the world after 1945 left France with the status of a secondary power in an international system where Soviet-American domination seemed unchallenged. With the fall of the Berlin wall, the victory of the United States in the absence of any opponent that could match it led to a unipolar era in which France was set, a priori, to play a marginal role. Nevertheless, in both cases, France went to great lengths to break out of the inconsequential position for which it seemed destined. To this end, it summoned up the classic and diverse means of the powerful, from nuclear weapons through to industrial policy or even the promotion of language. France's policy in Africa is in keeping with this framework. The consistency with which the different governments of the Fifth Republic worked to preserve and reinforce the ties between the former colonial power and the newly independent states is less accounted for by reasons specific to Africa than by the ideological foundations which governed the implementation of its global foreign policy. French elites actually share among themselves an identical vision of France in the world which can basically be summarised as the permanent search for a place among the most powerful in the international system. This search, which sometimes may seem to border on an obsession, permeates French policy in Africa and explains the particularity as well as the continuity of the measures which France has exhibited in sub-Saharan Africa. Only the end of bipolarity led it to reconsider these. Nevertheless, this revision did not signal a renunciation of the wish to rank first among the great powers in the evolving international system. The reformulation of France's Africa policy thus appeared to be substantial in measure but remarkably continuous as far as its underlying principles are concerned. In many ways exceptionalist, French policy in Africa serves to perpetuate France's self-awareness of exceptionalism.

THE COLD WAR, AFRICA, AND FRENCH EXCEPTIONALISM

Cold War logic was based on exclusion. It left no space beyond the ascendancy of the two superpowers. France's whole diplomatic art would lie in skirting round this law underlying an international system of exceptional rigidity, introducing flexibility where implicit rules tended to congeal situations.

Surviving defeat

After the Second World War France found itself in a paradoxical situation – at once conqueror and conquered. Behind the façade of a country whose sovereignty had been rehabilitated, an actor in the final negotiations of 1945, member of the UN Security Council, a less glorious reality was hiding. France was at best a secondary power. The United States and the Soviet Union personified the new masters of an evolving international system within which the old European powers, France, the United Kingdom and Germany, of course, were destined for subordination. An aggravating factor, still faltering decolonisation, risked removing the most visible attributes of the extended power, the Empire. Unlike the United Kingdom, which could hope to continue living its fallen power status by proxy through the United States, France found itself alone. This refusal to be reduced to playing a secondary role implied the necessity of activating its available resources. In this regard sub-Saharan Africa offered unrivalled opportunities. It had been due to its colonial empire that France was able to continue existing during the war even though its metropolitan part had been occupied, and sub-Saharan Africa was conspicuous in its loyalty to the empire. Through the impetus given by Félix Eboué, the first ruler to side with General de Gaulle since 1940, the entire sub-Saharan Africa shifted to a rejection of the Vichy government. The same Félix Eboué was at the Brazzaville conference, which, in January 1944, created the French Union that opened the door to the gradual integration of the colonies in lieu of granting them independence.

The specificity of sub-Saharan Africa continued to reinforce this close relationship. Africa south of the Sahara was spared the shocks that were reverberating across the colonial empire. The events at Sétif in Algeria and those in Madagascar, the wars of Indochina then of Algeria, the liberation of the protectorates of Tunisia and then Morocco, gave expression to the growing cracks in the French colonial system. Sub-Saharan Africa, for its part, continued to affirm its loyalty. Besides, its elites were hardly inclined to call for independence. For Houpouët-Boigny, Léon Mba, Diori Hamani ... the desire for black Africans to be citizens of France, prevailed. The African Democratic Assembly, which brought together the bulk of African representatives in the French parliament, argued for an improvement in social and political conditions (abolishment of forced labour, right to vote, and the abolition of the dual school system), but still within the framework of the French Union. The 1956 Deferre framework law did not alter the facts: it put the emphasis on Africa's necessary development and the broadening of mechanisms that would allow Africans to participate in social and political life. The community created in 1958 expressed this 'French desire', which was then widely shared by those south of the Sahara. Responding to an inescapable independence as a result of changes in the international environment, the community was conceived of as a construction that would allow for independence while remaining within the fold of the former colonial power. It is the famous 'independence in interdependence' that epitomises the depth of the ties between France and sub-Saharan Africa and the refusal to detach from these. What was needed was Sékou Touré's refusal in 1958 to derail the train of the community and to lead sub-Saharan Africa towards an independence around which the actors seemed to have rallied by default. The onus was on them to reconstruct this particular relation according to new modalities while retaining its spirit.

HINTERLAND AND DIVISION OF LABOUR

The conviction that Africa is necessary for France whereas the latter still claims a role for itself in world affairs did not disappear with independence. To the contrary, with the bipolar logic asserting itself, France discovered the rules of the international game and adapted to them. If it could no longer pretend to play directly at the 'centre' of the international system where the law of the superpowers excluded any third actor, it had at its disposal a margin of action at the periphery. France's artistry would lie in carving out for itself a distinctive zone of influence, which without going against the bipolar logic, would allow it to play its score and thus punch way above the weight conferred on it by the French territory alone in international relations.

The former colonies were integrated into a new institutional body, which in many respects was a product of the construction of a neo-colonial mechanism. The structures put into place directly affected sovereign state prerogatives. In the monetary area, the CFA franc allowed France partly to prolong its control of African economic space but especially to confer the status of an international currency on the French franc. In the same way that a dollar zone or a yen zone exists, a franc zone exists. As such, independence did not fundamentally change the rules of the game insofar as the French franc was able to assert itself as a legacy of the colonial period. When in 1945, Minister of Finances, René Pléven, called for the formation of an African currency linked to the French franc, he justified this step by the necessity to fight against the risk of 'dollarisation' experienced in Africa since the French retirement during the Second World War. The function of the CFA franc was made explicit: beyond the monetary advantages members were supposed to gain from belonging to the zone, it was a matter of making piecemeal of the hegemony of the dollar and therefore the United States and thus affirming French power.[1] More precisely it was to reject the bipolar hegemony as François Mitterand explained very precociously in 1953: 'From the Congo to the Rhine, the third nation-continent will balance itself around our metropolis.'[2] Bipolarity was not a fate, but a constraint whose stranglehold it was up to France to undo in order to endeavour substituting for it ... tripolarity. Without doubt that was more a matter of wishful thinking than a measured stocktaking of the international reality. At the very least, the vision conveyed by the one who became president of the Republic less than two decades later expressed the state of mind inhabiting the bulk of the French ruling class, the left-leaning Gaullists: the bipolar international structure should not lead France to abdicate its power.

Military co-operation reinforced this French search for influence measuring up to its ambitions. The technical military assistance agreements signed with 23 countries south of the Sahara and the defence pacts constituted a very comprehensive package. Through it France was given the capacity to intervene in the area of African states' security at the same time as its was provided with the knowledge of the internal security structure of each of the states taking part in the agreements. This right to look was in some way guaranteed by the clauses that were held secret and which linked certain African states to France and under whose terms France could be solicited to participate in operations to maintain order within the states seeking assistance. Thanks to the troops said to number around 10 000 men, France set itself up as a de facto policeman of Africa, to use the recognised expression. If taken literally, this expression may appear excessive, without doubt. Still, the fact remains that France has intervened very regularly in countries south of the Sahara since 1962 to restore a head of state threatened by internal conflicts (Gabon in 1964, Zaire in 1977–1978) or regimes harmed by foreign ambitions, with the defence of Chad's territory in the face of Libyan incursions thought to be the most revealing example in this regard.[3] These different interventions illustrate the remarks of former French Foreign Minister, Louis de Guiringaud, declaring in 1975: 'Africa is the only place where France can, with 500 men, change the course of history.' In other words, thanks to Africa, France has a field at its disposition which allows it to behave like a great power regionally without really being one globally, even though the income from Africa has given it some weight in international institutions. At the UN, France 'controls', through the African states affiliated to it, between a fifth and a sixth of the votes in the General Assembly. Moreover, equipped with its veto at the Security Council, it had a decisive ability to influence the entire UN system. The United States still does not view this overvalued French presence at the UN in a favourable light. But bipolar logic would lead them to compromise in the case in point.

The status of a great power in Africa, which France had built up for itself, would in fact be officially sanctioned by the United States in the framework of a functional division of labour. Guaranteeing the security of African states belonging to the hinterland, France was simultaneously responsible for anchoring them to the West. The regimes tempted by the appeal of the eastern bloc would be progressively stifled, be it Sékou Touré's Guinea, Modhibo Keita's Mali or even, albeit more slowly, Madagascar. Some would content themselves with succumbing to the charms of the Marxist-Leninist discourse, following the example of Mathieu Kéréko in Benin or Marian Ngouabi in Congo, but without their rhetorical options finding expression in an explicit pro-Soviet policy. To the contrary, their closeness to France would be carefully cultivated, each knowing exactly how advantageous French co-operation policy was through its different mechanisms. According to the classical pattern of political exchange, each of the actors saw its interests being satisfied. The United States granted France its status as a great power in Africa in exchange for which France provided the maintenance, militarily, economically, and financially of western order in the region. As for the African states, they were given freedom of ideological choice and internal political practice on condition that they remained in the French fold. In return, France guaranteed them the benefit of its co-operation and its protection both externally and internally. Placed at the intersection between American and African interests, France maximised its own gains by gradually extending its hinterland beyond the initial sphere. Extending beyond the borders inherited from French West Africa and Equatorial French Africa (the so-called sphere countries, according to the terminology used in the French Ministry of Co-operation) Paris progressively integrated the peripheral states 'conquered' from former Belgian (Zaire, Rwanda, Burundi), Spanish (Equatorial Guinea) and Portuguese possessions.[4] The only fly in the ointment in this enlargement of the French sphere of influence was the failure of the Biafra secession, which France supported in the hope of weakening the giant Anglophone Nigeria in West Africa.

Impossible transformation

The benefits derived by France from its Africa policy explain the resistance with which the vague desires or necessity for change was met. For this policy has shown that it had not been exempt from being dysfunctional. Its implementation through different co-operation instruments too often degenerated into a vast clientilistic enterprise, diverting the means from their initial objectives. The development imperative, which gave France's Africa policy its *cause noblesse*, has been eroded progressively, reducing the French presence to a mere search for power while simultaneously arbitrating a multitude of interests, public or private, without any link to the proclaimed philosophy. This acknowledgement, reiterated time and again, including in official reports, has nevertheless not been followed to any tangible effect. To the contrary, far from transforming itself, French policy in Africa revelled in its habits, successfully applying itself to block any initiative for change.

It would be a fastidious undertaking to draw up the list of grievances because non-governmental organisations, universities and different public authorities have done so already. The significance lies in a convergence of the diagnosis, which boils down to the contrast between the original intelligence and generosity and the reality, according to Alain Vivien in his 1990 report commissioned by the French government.[5] This reality was made up of spoilt projects, 'white elephants',[6] and loans made in such a way that the 40bn francs spent annually on public development assistance were hardly effective. It was on these grounds that Franco-African networks proliferated, linking politicians and political parties, state enterprises, private companies, information services and bureaucratic systems. In this conglomeration only the initiated could find their way. Every ministry was bestowed with a competency to deal with African matters – the most significant being the Ministries of Economy and Finances, Co-operation, and Defence. The Ministry of Foreign Affairs also played a central role but without the power to pose as the co-ordinating instrument of different institutional actors as would normally be the case. France's Africa policy, therefore, has been conceived according to a specific exceptionalist mechanism. The overall architecture was complicated by the particular place it has held under the Fifth Republic.

With General de Gaulle and his African affairs advisor, Jacques Foccart, Africa was raised to the specific domain of the head of state. The famous African committee on the Elysée draws its reputation, often derogatory, from its untypical nature. Led by a personality who reported only to the president, it was both an official and secret body. 'Mister Africa' who was responsible for it found himself at the intersection between different actors and different institutions involved in African policy, both in France and in sub-Saharan Africa. More than any other, he personified this policy, maintaining direct relations with African heads of state who knew that they were in fact dealing directly with the head of state through his intermediary. This relationship of confidence, unique in state-to-state relationships, inaugurated by Jacques Foccart, lasted without a break throughout the Fifth Republic, culminating at the very time of François Mitterand's second seven-year term in the nomination of his own son, Jean-Christophe to head up this committee.[7] Nevertheless, continuing this African policy under a presidential system which follows the logic of the more general executive style of foreign policy and is in keeping with the so-called 'reserved domain' doctrine has not prevented institutional segmentation to have its effects. Incidences of bureaucratic competition have multiplied and become entrenched over time, in the purest style of the 'stay-at-home conquerors', denounced by Alain

Vivien in his report.[8] Each ministerial department was busy defending its administrative 'territory'. The Ministry of the Economy, which managed both the CFA franc via the Treasury Directorate, but also the largest share of the development funds intended for debt management and support of the budgets of African states, had no intention whatsoever of relinquishing its hegemonic position. The Ministry of Co-operation, valued for its development assistance funds via the Aid and Co-operation Fund, was buttressing its domain, afraid of being crushed between the Ministries of Economy and Finance on the one side, and the Ministry of Foreign Affairs on the other. The latter did not take kindly to the African exception from the 'sphere', which took away its role as general architect of all of France's foreign relations. The Ministry of Defence, for its part, saw in Africa a parading ground allowing for the type of rehearsals that would be impossible in times of peace (the operations in Chad were rather significant in this scheme), a resource allowing it to have a capacity to influence French strategic decisions particularly through its information services, and, more trivially, a means of improving career progress thanks to the rotation of troops that had already been positioned and the primacy attached to this. Any attempt at reform would therefore come up against firm resistance, despite the deadlocks into which African policy progressively became tied.

Its economic efficiency proved doubtful. When François Mitterrand became president of the Republic in 1981, conditions seemed favourable for a thorough revision of the French system. Not only did the discourse of the left argue in this direction, but rigorous analysis of this policy hardly favoured its maintenance. Economically, it did not really contribute to a reversal of African economic decline. Co-operation has neither led to nor accompanied development even though this was its basic justification. The French economy from its side seemed to have profited from its trade with Africa: it showed a surplus industrial balance. On the other hand, as the Berthelot-De Bandt report noted, this benefit should not be considered as a necessarily favourable indicator to the extent to which it hides the deterioration of the competitiveness of the French economy. African economies, actually, were hardly dynamic and in its relations with them, France had specific advantages linked to the French zone and the automatic spin-offs from public development assistance. Whichever point of view one considers, that of Africa or that of France, there seems to be no doubt. Politically, this picture is hardly optimistic. All the African regimes in the French zone were characterised by their authoritarianism, with the exception of Senegal, where even a tempered liberalism could hardly qualify this statement. Everywhere the arbitrary and systematic violation of human rights was holding sway. More seriously, the patrimonisation of African states, brought about by a systematic confusion between the public and private domains, have corrupted actors and practices in France.

The reforms suggested by the Minister of Co-operation and Development, Jean-Pierre Cot, in 1982 were therefore produced in a particularly favourable context. Wishing to reconcile doctrine and efficiency, the French minister suggested that Africa be dissolved from the special sphere of influence into the much larger third world grouping. The minister of co-operation was thus given the general task of development assistance to all the countries of the south of which Africa, by definition, was only one component. Institutionally, this enlargement meant the integration of 'Monsieur' Street in Quai d'Orsay. This reform in fact was revolutionary. It immediately aroused hostility within the circle of African leaders ... and various French actors, all who had been part of a system that nourished their particular interests, albeit in an often conflicting manner. Less than a year later, the reforms were laid aside and Jean-Pierre Cot had been persuaded to resign. Nevertheless, to explain this retraction as the result of the crosscutting game of many actors implicated in the functioning of the French-African complex, worsened by the African lack of appreciation of the reformist minister and his advisors, which is the most commonly held view, is overlooking the main cause. The major reason why this reform was impossible was the bipolar rationality and the role France came to attribute to itself pinned in between the two superpowers. Would not the implementation of these reforms have destroyed what all governments in Paris have patiently conceived and constructed since the end of the Second World War? In favouring continuity over reform, François Mitterand again took up the flame of an African policy that has been condemned to live on until such time as the very conception of the role France has assigned itself in the world is reconsidered.

THE CONFLAGRATION OF BERLIN: REINVENTED EXCEPTIONALISM

French African policy, its foundations and advantages all lumped together, was brutally propelled into a new world. The fall of the Berlin wall caused a shock wave that split through the entire international system. In Africa, the upheaval took the shape of a questioning of authoritarianism by African populations themselves. Protest movements that until then had been systematically repressed by African leaders embarked upon uncertain political ventures named 'transition' by default. Shaken, the entire French system in sub-Saharan Africa had to be revised. For lack of having been thought through, this operation was going to be improvised, discovering obstacles and resistance as it went along. It would only become coherent once the new international politics had been digested and a substitute doctrine, adapted to the post-bipolar world, would redefine French exceptionalism in Africa.

Do-it-yourself and follow-the-leader

Franco-African summits arose according to the classical formula of the Grand Army mess. They allowed for the annual celebration of particular Franco-African friendships according to an immutable ritual: the French head of state, surrounded by African heads of states or their representatives, ranked in order of seniority, would deliver a speech whose content never changed. In it the past would be recalled, it would ponder the present and predict the future. This was hardly a dangerous exercise as long as the framework of this collective thinking was marked out. History, beautiful and generous, was summoned to recall the exceptional human richness of the patrimony all had in common. The injustice of the North-South division allowed them to face up to an enemy that was all the more fearsome because it was everywhere. And France would underline its unique co-operation effort, which each of them willingly conceded. All this was in an appeasing and familial tone.[9] In short, everyone at these summits agreed on almost everything for any subject that could cause anger was avoided. Also, when in June 1990, on the occasion of the La Baule summit, the French president launched into an apology of pluralism and the link between development aid and political reform, his speech provoked some gnashing of teeth. When looked at more closely, however, the revolution appeared less devastating than what a hasty reading of the presidential text would suggest. Though François Mitterrand underlined the universality of democracy and the beneficial effects of freedom for African societies, he moderated his remarks by making clear that France had no intention to 'dictate any constitutional law whatsoever that would de facto impose upon an entire people that have their conscience and their own culture'.[10] This did not diminish the fact that La Baule was an abrupt change in the "good child" tone of previous summits. In reality, France had its back against the wall, was caught in a whirlpool of events that it did not control and which it was trying hard to catch hold of. In Africa, Benin kicked off a process, through the challenging of Matthieu Kérékou, which spread throughout the countries in France's sphere of influence. National summits became contagious. Their results would be mixed and uneven, but, at the time of the La Baule summit, France was forced to take into account events over which it hardly had any hold.

The months that followed would bring to the fore French ambivalence, hesitating between explicit support for 'democratic transitions' and an evolution that risked causing the implosion of sub-Saharan regimes and leaving behind the consolidated model of Franco-African relations. Faced with the new situation, French leaders, for lack of a clearly defined line of approach, hesitated, caught between idealism, recalled by some intellectuals and hardliners, and realism, in many ways behaving spinelessly. The legislative elections in the spring of 1993 emphasised the confusion insofar as they embarked on a second cohabitation, which hardly predisposed them to rash initiatives. What was more, the proximity of the 1995 presidential elections, against the background of the battle for the candidature between, on the right, the Prime Minister, Edouard Balladur and the head of the RPR, Jacques Chirac, brought to a standstill any prospects of reform. Africa, already second on the political agenda, found itself relegated to the ranks of those questions destined for a long wait. The French opposition to change proved to be hardly on the same wavelength as immediate African history, which continued to run its course. On 11 January 1994 one of the pillars of the Franco-African system imploded: the CFA franc was devalued by 50 per cent. This development demanded change, even though government circles remained in favour of continuity.[11]

French officials actually never anticipated the devaluation of the CFA franc. The fixed exchange rate had been raised to an absolute guarantee, symbolic of France's indestructible attachment to its former colonies, but also a sign of its power. Whatever the economic performance of the African states that were members of the franc zone countries group, France was assuring them a stable exchange rate, which had substantial benefits notably in terms of access to major currency markets. The immutable character of this parity was part of the post-colonial pact that linked

France to those African states in its sphere of influence. Any allusion to an eventual change in parity signified the violation of a taboo. Nevertheless, this assurance was illusory insofar as it implied that France had a unilateral capacity to correct and fill the growing gap between the value of the currency and the real economy of these African states. Such a system took neither the disparities between the franc zone countries and other African economies with which they still traded, most especially Nigeria, nor the disparities between countries inside the zone, nor the effects of economic globalisation, which imposed a permanent currency adjustment between them, into account. All these elements should have been taken into account long before. They were known; their effects could be foreseen. But economic logic had to step aside before the primacy of political rationality, whatever deadlocks this may have led to. For lack of having been thought through, the devaluation was similar to a surrendering of French power in the face of superior forces, made worse by the feeling of desertion and betrayal then prevailing in the countries of the hinterland.[12] Incapable of shaping the future of African by itself, contrary to the myth it had fostered consistently, France was reduced to follow along the new market democracy rules dictated by the international Bretton Woods institutions.

Two lines

Jolted by events, paralysed by internal political factors, intellectually ossified, France proved incapable of breathing coherence into its Africa policy. The election of Jacques Chirac to the presidency of the Republic in 1995 cleared the landscape by making an official division between two possible conceptions of France's Africa policy:[13] those who held on to the status quo and those who supported the modernisation of all the institutions involved in managing the French-African relationship.

The debate seemed to have been settled with the arrival of Jacques Chirac at the Elysée insofar as he declared right away that he was convinced of the need for a radical change in France's Africa policy.[14] Taking such a position seemed to reinforce the policy that was already being implemented in the economic arena. The conditionality that François Mitterand announced at the La Baule summit was put into effect under the government of Edouard Balladur in the form of the so-called Abidjan doctrine set out in 1994. Straight in line with devaluation, which he had to take on, the

French prime minister established a distinction between project aid that applied to development programmes and non-project aid that concerned balancing the budget and macro-economic stability. Edouard Balladur indicated that for the latter, French aid would be conditional on a prior agreement between African states and the IMF. As IMF aid was the more significant in volume, this explanation did not concern itself with details. What it did was to inscribe French aid policy within the framework of the rules of conditionality. As such, it acknowledged that the principles of structural adjustment were well founded and that the Bretton Woods institutions were supreme in defining the new principles that would guide France's Africa policy. At the end of 1994, the Minister of Economic Affairs, Edmond Alphandery, called for order for the benefit of African states, some of whom wanted to free themselves from the constraints of adjustment by signing mere 'reference programmes' with the IMF. The nomination of Alain Juppé at Matignon as Jacques Chirac's prime minister corresponded to the acceleration of the rationalisation process already under way. Strengthened by presidential support, the new premier undertook a major reform of co-operation and development assistance, which had by then amounted to an annual cost of 40 billion francs. The overall savings of this project were based on concentrating all the institutions responsible for development in the Quai d'Orsay. The Ministry of Co-operation would be amalgamated with the Ministry of Foreign Affairs. France's external economic activities were also to fall within the scope of the latter's responsibilities, which ended up placing the Ministry of Economic Affairs, which managed three-quarters of all development assistance, under the control of diplomats. The establishment of a Development Agency allowed for a shake-up of the crumbling administrative apparatus, which had a propensity for disorder and chaos. Finally, with the minister of foreign affairs having been set up to orchestrate this radical reorganisation, there ensued a dilution of the hinterland Africa policy into a resolutely continental conception of African policy.

This upheaval crashed headlong into the logic of the traditional Franco-African complex, as it had previously in 1982. This complex, defended by among others Minister of Co-operation, Jacques Godfrain, but also by Jacques Foccart, who returned to African affairs as 'official' advisor to the president, called for maintaining differential treatment to the countries of the sphere of influence, in the name of France's African friendships and well understood French interests. In the case in point, this conservative current was situated within some continuity of the

Mitterrand policy. President Mitterrand had had the opportunity to tone down his remarks from La Baulle during the Biarritz Franco-African summit in November 1994, when he vilified 'the inspired prophets responsible for dictating to African peoples what was best for them'.[15] The mobilisation of networks still attached to continuity succeeded in convincing President Chirac to postpone reform, which was officially buried at the end of 1995 at the Benin *'francophonie'* summit. The announcement that an 'independent' Co-operation Ministry 'with its own means and identity' would be maintained reassured African leaders and largely emptied this project, credited to Alain Juppé, of its content.[16] The difficulty of thinking about African policy beyond the habitual categories was cruelly confirmed by the shock caused by the information which emerged in the wake of the Rwandan genocide perpetrated between April and June 1994. The support for the regime of President Habyarimana, the involvement of the French army in tasks that seemed to have been little more than a mere military co-operation mission, the blindness of French decision makers, diplomatic and political, all pointed out that France had acted according to principles inspired by an antiquated conception of France south of the Sahara, worsened by Anglo-Saxon phobia[17] and polluted by the secret game of networks woven through the web of French-African relations. The incredible episode of the French mercenary, Bob Denard, in the Comoros in the autumn of 1995 for its part brought to light that the 'twisted coup' was ruled by clans that were still operating at the very inside of the French state and in defiance of the latter insofar as the interested party was under French juridical control when he overthrew the regime of President Djohar.[18] When President Mobutu was officially received in Paris in April 1996 and it was announced that co-operation with Zaire would be resumed, continuity, prevailed over change.

AMERICAN 'HYPER-POWER', FRANCE, AND THE AFRICAN ARENA

Lacking any doctrine, France is struggling to maintain its position within the context of an African arena under reconstruction. The difficulty of imposing a firm political line in this domain stems from multiple factors as was demonstrated by the failure of the Juppé reforms. Numerous actors, not wanting in resources as much in Africa as in France, were still attached to the status quo.

The discontinuity of power linked to the clash of electoral, legislative or presidential obligations complicated the implementation of a policy that needed firmness and constancy. But above all, in order to break any final resistance, France needed a strategy that was sufficiently supported and likely to be convincing not only of the necessity for change but also of a cost-benefit relationship which did not elicit a feeling of a clear loss for France. From this perspective, the most difficult aspect for the French elites was to bid farewell to their backward-looking vision in which France still imagined itself as a big power with a universal calling faced with a power that was colossal but still threatened by the imperial temptation, namely the United States, a historical extension of the Anglo-Saxon enemy. The reading of power relations in the post-bipolar world, put forward by Minister of Foreign Affairs, Hubert Védrine, suggests a revision of the usual representation.[19] In substance, the minister in charge of French diplomacy suggested a three-level architecture of the international system. At the top level was the United States, which could qualify as a 'hyper-power' insofar as it was the only one which simultaneously held all the constituent elements of a great power. At the bottom level was the large mass of states that were lacking in the means with which effectively to carry some weight in international power relations. Between the two was a group of seven or eight states that were important powers. They did not simultaneously hold all resources, this was an American monopoly, but they had sufficient assets so that the hyper-power was not in a position of absolute domination. France was situated in this second group. It therefore had to renounce the nostalgia of great power that has been lost, but not give way to a disparaging perception of its reality either. The alternative was not between absolute and forfeited power, but between average and outmoded power. To assert itself as a middle power presupposes a rationalisation of means according to a hierarchical organisation of objectives. According to this perspective, France's African policy is costly and inappropriate to the African reality today and the gains that France is likely to obtain from it.

In its implementation, broadly France's African policy lies within the framework of the continuation of Alain Juppé's aborted reforms. The institutions in charge of African policy have been completely restructured. The Ministry of Co-operation is no longer a separate department. All that remains is a ministerial delegate in charge of a General Directorate for International Co-operation and Development. The other ministerial departments involved in

African policy (notably Defence and Finance) have been placed under the control of an Interministerial Committee for International Co-operation and Development. (CICID), linked directly to the prime minister and the minister of foreign affairs. Centring the institutional structure again around the head of government reduced the margin of action of those networks that fed off the autonomy of each state institution.[20] Other instruments of France's Africa policy had also been completely revised, particularly everything connected with French military capacity. Starting in 1996, pre-positioned troops saw their numbers reduced to 3 400 men, or nearly by a third.[21] This disengagement was balanced by the opening of military schools with a regional calling in Africa in order to train cadres of African armies on the spot and by setting up a programme called the Reinforcement of African Capacity to Maintain Peace (RECAMP) which aimed to transfer the mission of maintaining security south of the Sahara to African troops to whom France would supply the logistics.[22] Finally, the CFA franc, devalued, was promised a Europeanised future with the putting into place of the euro, which would help France avoid having to take charge of it alone. The new African policy therefore did not spare any foundation of African policy in its former version. The objective was evidently to reduce the costs to the French budget, as was confirmed by the constant decline in the total amount allotted to the public aid and development budget title after 1994, to the point where its value fell to the level of about twenty years ago.[23]

The direction taken by the French government was prompted by a strategy of gathering the means and rationalising their use. The beneficiaries were divided into two zones: the countries of the priority solidarity zone, essentially characterised by their poverty, and the countries of the economic partnership zone, which grouped together those countries which had an already asserted development potential. The first would be the privileged consignee of public aid, whereas the second would have priority access to the financial protocols and the private sector aid fund.

Put together, these arrangements paint a sensitively remodelled landscape where the means of power are calculated paradoxically to better marry the main themes of the new French power in Africa. This policy is resolutely continental and aims to reconcile its positioning in the dynamic zones, particularly southern Africa, without losing its influence in the countries of the former hinterland. Here, there is a priori little chance of giving meaning to a revitalised French exceptionlism. In fact, the entire logic of the strategy rests upon the idea according to which France remains the last power to show an interest in Africa and that, even with its diminished means, it would be able to exercise a unique position on the continent. President Clinton's trip to Africa marked the limits of American ambitions on the continent. Despite conforming to its hyper-power status as the enemy par excellence of France's interests south of the Sahara, the United States has nonetheless shown the limited attraction of extending its Africa policy. Evidently, with the demise of bipolarity, Washington no longer feels obliged to tolerate France's exclusivist aspirations towards continental Africa. Without doubt, that partly explains America's role in the Great Lakes or yet again the endless struggle in the United Nations to have Koffi Anan elected to the post of secretary general against Boutros-Boutros Ghali, considered above all France's 'man'. The American approach towards Africa was basically prompted by security considerations, as it manifested, for example, in the Sudan, or by economics. But, on this last point, its 'aid not trade' formula depends too much on the primacy of commerce in order to seduce, on a long-term basis, African states asking for development assistance, which is becoming scarce. This has resulted in a political and economic space that France thought it could occupy for itself. The November 1998 Franco-African summit in Paris illustrated this. By gathering together almost all the African states in Paris, France set itself up as the organising power of a post-bipolar African order. Nothing, however, indicates that in the end, this will be more efficient than in the past, not the least owing to the difficulties of regulating the conflicts tearing Africa apart solely through the mediation of the French power. Nothing indicates that the reduction of public aid will allow France to maintain acceptance of a French supremacy that is as accountable for its monies and conforms to the pervading mode which makes public aid an outmoded instrument in the countries of the former zone of influence. Nothing indicates that this rationalisation will not be perverted by the persistence of networks, shown to be alive by the complacency of the presidential election observer mission to Gabon at the end of 1998. In short, nothing indicates that Africa will constitute anew the last hope of a French power in search of itself. In the meanwhile, this Africa is allowing France to reinvent an exception for itself without which it would feel an orphan.

---

1 See Valleé Olivier, 'Le prix de l'argent CFA. Heurs et malherus de la zone franc', Paris, Karthala, 1989. See also the Observatoire Permanent de la Cooperation Française document, 'The devaluation of the CFA franc', in Rapport de l'OPCF, Paris, Desclée de Brouwer, 1995, pp 59–94.

2   See François Mitterand, 'Aux frontières de l'Union Française', Juillard, Indochina, Paris, Tunisia, 1953.
3   See the article by Anne-Sophie Boisgallais, 'Les derives de la cooperation militaire de la France en Afrique', OPCF Report, op.cit, pp 101–146 for all on French military co-operation.
4   The expansion of the hinterland happed without, for that matter, mechanistically deploying all instruments of French co-operation. The former Belgian and Portuguese colonies, therefore, would not be integrated into the CFA franc zone. But they benefited from Ministry of Co-operation funds.
5   Vivien Report, 1990, p 2.
6   According to a 1985 study, out of an identified range of 343 projects financed by the French budget, 195 were functioning very poorly and 79 have been stopped. For the French companies involved in these projects, the main thing was to carry out the initial work in order to benefit from public funding, without concern for the adequacy of these projects or the needs of the beneficiaries or to follow up the projects. On this see Eric Fottorino, Christophe Guillemin and Eric Orsenna, 'Besoin d'Afrique', Fayard, Paris, 1992.
7   The personalisation of France's Africa policy can be perfectly illustrated by the interviews of Jacques Foccart that appeared under the title 'Foccard talks: Interviews with Philippe Gaillard', Fayard, Paris, Volume 1, 1995, Volume 2 1997. Here, Jacques Foccart describes a good many scenes of receiving African heads of state at his personal residence, Luzerches, and stresses the 'familial' relations that tied him to the latter, notably as godfather of many of their children. Under François Mitterand, this familiarity was expressed in a humorous or ironic way with the nickname attached to Jean-Christophe Mitterand in African circles: Daddy told me ...
8   Alain Vivien, op.cit.
9   Calling people the familiar 'tu' instead of 'vous' in French was the done thing. Where François Mitterand never let go to this extent, Jacques Chirac, on the other hand, took to this very spontaneously. On this point see Stephen Smith, 'La doctrine Africaine de Chirac: Les mots clés du nouveau discours présidentiel', *Libération*, 20 July 1995.
10 *Le Monde*, 22 June, 1990.
11 On continuity and change in France's African policy, see Tony Chafer, 'French African policy: towards change', *African Affairs*, Vol 91, 1992, and Guy Martin, 'Continuity and change in Franco-African relations, *Journal of Modern African Studies*, Vol 33(1), 1995, pp 1–20.
12 On the devaluation, see the OPCF Report, op.cit., and more particularly Daniel Bourmaud, 'France-l'Afrique: l'implosion', pp 81–94. The feeling of betrayal expressed by many African elites had to do, beyond the surprise of the devaluation, with the conditions under which this was decided in Dakar.
13 On all these aspects see Daniel Bourmaud, 'La politique africaine de Jacques Chirac: les Anciens contre les Modernes', Modern and Contemporary France, 1994, NS4 (4), pp 431–42.
14 'Everything needs to change, we need to put an end to autocratic and corrupted heads of state', he would have declared after getting to know about a report on corruption of African elite leaders. On this subject see Antoine Glaser and Stephen Smith, 'Deux lignes africaines pour la France', *Libération*, 25 June 1995.
15 Jeune Afrique Economique, December 1994, p 29.
16 Libération, 4 December 1995.
17 See Gérard Prunier, 'The Rwanda crisis: 1959–1994 – history of a genocide', Hrust and Company, 1995, for a history of the events in Rwanda.
18 On this subject, see 'Affaires des Comoros. Les secrets d'un coup tordu', Le Point, 6 January 1996.
19 Interview in the Nouvel Observateur, No 1751, 28 May 1998.
20 Le Figaro, 29 January 1999.
21 *Libération*, 1 December 1995.
22 This new conception of African security was implemented in February 1999 in Guinea Bissau. See *Libération*, 29 January 1999.
23 See Daniel Bourmaud, 'La'aide publique au dévéloppement. Les moyens de la fin?', *Observatoire Permanent de la Coopération Française, Rapport 1998*, Paris, Karthala, 1998.

Chapter Two:

SOUTH AFRICA IN AFRICA: THE APARTHEID REGIME'S FOREIGN POLICY IN SUB-SAHARAN AFRICA[1]

Roger Southall

Prior to 1994, much analysis of South Africa's foreign policy in Africa was conducted in overwhelmingly ideological terms. The maintenance of apartheid was viewed as incompatible with 'white' South Africa enjoying collaborative and stable relations with 'black' Africa.[2] The strength of this approach was that it focussed upon the peculiarity and particularity of South African foreign policy. The assumption of conventional foreign policy analysis was that governments pursued an identifiably 'national interest' in the international sphere; in contrast, South African foreign policy was viewed as designed to promote and maintain white minority rule, even if (confusingly) some analysts chose to define it as an expression of the national security interests of the Afrikaner people.[3] The threat perceived by Afrikaners or whites of being overwhelmed by the black majority was translated into a fundamental opposition to African nationalism, whatever pragmatic accommodations with African governments' developments in the region and the continent were, in practice, to require.

In practice, some analysts looked beyond apartheid as an ideology to explain South African foreign policy behaviour. For instance, Kenneth Grundy acknowledged 'the intransmutability of race as a primary determining factor in intra-state and inter-state political relations', but insisted that because emphasis upon doctrine could also obfuscate policy, it was necessary to map out underlying realities which shaped state behaviour. These included, notably, the economic and transport links between the countries of southern Africa which predated and coexisted with apartheid. It was the economic patterns that had emerged from the colonial milieu which set the tone for the perception of political alternatives upon which foreign policies were based. And South African economic hegemony was by far the most 'imposing structural characteristic' determining southern African affairs, persuading some African governments to become 'bridge builders', and others to ameliorate their hostility to Pretoria.[4]

Taking the lead from Grundy, I attempted in the early 1980s to move beyond the study of South Africa's foreign policy as designed principally to ensure 'white survival' by examining it as an expression of the dynamics of the South African political economy throughout the post-Second World War years. I divided this era into three periods: (i) the consolidation of state capitalism, 1948–61; (ii) state partnership with monopoly capital, 1961–76; and (iii) fissure and crisis of the apartheid state, 1976 to the present. I argued that this characterisation corresponded with the three broad phases in South African foreign policy, namely (i) resistance and adjustment to Africa's decolonisation; (ii) the Republic's emergence as a 'sub-imperial' power; and (iii) a transition from détente with neighbouring black Africa to its destabilisation.[5] The continual assertion of the primacy of the apartheid ideological factor by conventional foreign policy analysts tended to diminish the other determinants of foreign policy behaviour in the region. In this chapter, I will argue that economic factors underpinned South Africa's Africa policy, although it is evident that these were to become subordinate to military and strategic imperatives as apartheid became subject to mounting pressure during the final years of its existence.

THE APARTHEID STATE 1948–61: RESPONSE TO AFRICAN DECOLONISATION

The development of the white settler society in South Africa was founded upon violent conquest and was encouraged by British imperial interests for commercial reasons. It also included the massive appropriation of land, the exploitation of black labour, the extraction of mineral wealth and, from the mid-1920s, the adoption of policies of protectionism, which fostered the rapid development of secondary industrialisation. The South African political economy was founded upon a broad compatibility of metropolitan (imperial) and national (settler) interests after the granting of political independence via the formation of Union in 1910. However, there were major changes within the white society, which emanated from the rise of an Afrikaner nationalist bourgeoisie. The economic muscle of this bourgeoisie lay in an ethnic mobilisation of capital in the inter-war years and their control of state capital after the victory of the National Party (NP) in the general election of 1948. The NP was founded upon an alliance of a disadvantaged Afrikaner bourgeoisie, which was primarily located in agriculture and small-scale manufacturing, and the Afrikaner working class opposing the United Party (UP), led by General Smuts, and which represented the interests of financial, mining, large-scale and thus 'English' capital. The NP came into office committed to the programme of apartheid, and promised the fruits of racial dominance to its key constituents.[6]

Subsequently, apartheid legislation increased the emphasis of racial segregation in social life and the suppression of political opposition which represented a serious challenge to NP rule, culminating in the banning of the African National Congress (ANC) and Pan-Africanist Congress (PAC) in 1961. It also included the codification and extension of a highly coercive system of control, the regulation of the African labour force through the migrant labour system, and the abolition of all African political rights in the central polity in favour of the 'separate development' of ethnically differentiated 'homelands' for the African population. This latter aspect eventually developed into a programme of quasi-decolonisation, whereby the 'bantustans' were propelled through successive states of 'self-government' culminating in juridical sovereignty and 'independence' for Transkei, Bophuthatswana, Venda and Ciskei (TBVC).

The state apparatus was used to promote Afrikaner interests throughout the political economy. In the 1950s, the NP government embarked upon an expansion of the public sector, which promoted the Afrikaner economic advance. A number of parastatals, such as the Iron and Steel Corporation (ISCOR) and the Industrial Development Corporation (IDC) had been established before 1948, but after the NP came to power there was an increase in direct state involvement in the economy. This included the creation of a wide array of agricultural control boards and public enterprises, such as the Electricity Supply Commission (ESCOM), the Armaments Corporation of South Africa, (ARMSCOR) and the Phosphate Development Corporation (FOSKOR). A distinct feature of their development was their employment of Afrikaner personnel. This was instrumental in diminishing English and foreign control of the economy and in expanding secondary industry and making the country less reliant on mining. The development of state capitalism and the rapid growth of the economy significantly increased Afrikaner participation in the private sector and contributed to a marked upward mobility of the Afrikaner population in the occupational sphere.

After 1948, the NP's foreign policy involved a redefinition of South Africa's relations with the Commonwealth, which revolved around the growing commitment of Britain to the decolonisation of its African colonies. South Africa's pre-war foreign relations had been dominated by two conflicting traditions. The first, embodied by General Smuts, expressed a commitment to a joint South African (white) nationhood, and an active participation in international affairs as a sovereign state within the Commonwealth. Indeed, South Africa was regarded as a key military and industrial base, 'a link in the Commonwealth chain of defence whenever Africa was threatened by outside powers'.[7] The second, developed by the Nationalists under General Hertzog in opposition in the 1930s, was isolationist and interpreted Afrikaner nationhood as requiring the severing of formal political links with the British crown. But Smuts's vision was doomed not only by the NP's rise to power in 1948, but by the post-war transformation of the Commonwealth from a club of white dominions into a *multiracial* ensemble of states. The establishment of the United Nations (UN) in 1945, the granting of independence to India, and the subsequent commitment by Britain to the decolonisation of its African colonies signified a commitment to racial equality to which the new South African government was opposed. This made apartheid the focal point of increasing international criticism.

However, the NP's commitment to republicanism was tempered by the potential costs of isolation. Smuts had played a major role in the founding of the UN, but the NP became increasingly resentful of that body as it became a forum for anti-apartheid criticism. South Africa proved particularly resistant to claims that its legal right to govern South West Africa, today Namibia, the former German colony which the Union had administered since 1921 under the League of Nations mandate, was invalidated because its racial policies contravened the UN's Charter of Rights. Although the International Court of Justice ruled in 1950 that the League's mandate was still in force, the government refused to recognise any right of UN supervision. However, although the South West Africa Amendment Act of 1949 granted whites their first direct representation in the Union's parliament, the government remained wary of the international complications which would follow full legal incorporation of the territory.

In a post-Second World War world, which South Africa viewed as menaced by the communist threat, a major objective of the government was to gain admission to a western defensive alliance. It directed a special effort towards securing an agreement concerning the defence of the African continent. However, because South Africa declined to be party to any agreement which involved the bearing of arms by black troops, and because the western powers were dubious of the posited communist danger to the continent, no African alliance was formed. In addition, both France and Britain were beginning to query their stay as colonial powers in Africa, and were becoming worried about the international opprobrium that a formal defensive link with Pretoria would incur. The Simonstown Agreement of 1955, which gave the British Navy the use of facilities in the Cape lent substance to the charge that Britain was in league with apartheid. South Africa's retention of Commonwealth membership therefore compensated in part for the country's exclusion from other international groupings. India's accession to republican status within the Commonwealth opened up a similar option for the Union. But the declaration of a republic, even after a referendum, would have divided the whites, while outright departure from the Commonwealth risked reducing Pretoria's influence over Britain's Africa policy, and implied the loss of imperial preference for South Africa's trade goods in a world increasingly hostile to apartheid.

Despite these diplomatic estrangements, relations with the West were strengthened throughout the 1950s by an extension of economic links. South Africa emerged from the war with large financial reserves, and these were considerably augmented by a large capital inflow from Britain. This enhanced a high level of investment by both the private sector and the rapidly expanding parastatals. The consequent development of the manufacturing sector, which had received a major boost from the war, not only extended overseas links, but also diversified South Africa's international contacts, notably with Europe and the United States. South Africa had long been the world's largest supplier of gold, but industrial growth in the advanced capitalist economies fuelled demand for the country's wealth in other minerals: chromium, platinum group metals, manganese, vanadium, asbestos, vermiculite, iron, coal, uranium, diamonds and copper. The export of these minerals was not only instrumental in redressing the imbalance of trade in other commodities, but also in forging stronger ties with mineral-consuming countries, many of which were in significant measure dependent upon South Africa for their supplies of scarce materials. If the decline of the British empire required that territories to the north be conceded to the uncertainties of African rule, the prospect of continuing white supremacy served to increase, rather than diminish, South Africa's attraction to external investors.

South Africa was strongly opposed to all prospects of decolonisation. Hardened by Portugal's resolve to maintain control over Angola and Mozambique, Pretoria became progressively dismayed by Britain's prevarications and eventual decision to withdraw from Africa. Initially, South African politicians deemed it inconceivable that Britain could hand over power to independent black states. Indeed, Prime Minister Malan's flotation of an 'African Charter', which was committed to the protection of Africa against Asian, notably Indian, and communist domination and to the preservation of western civilisation, was necessarily premised upon continuing colonial rule. The most immediate concern was to ensure continuing white hegemony over southern Africa. In 1953, the two Rhodesias had been joined with Nyasaland in the Central African Federation, in part to 'resist the fatal southward pull of Malan's Nationalist Union', whose manufacturing industries found a ready market for their goods in all three countries.[8] If the subsequent development of nationalism in Northern Rhodesia (Zambia) and Nyasaland (Malawi) was in considerable degree a struggle against political domination by the white settlers in their southern neighbour, South Africa was steadfast in its commitment to upholding white rule in Southern Rhodesia as a bulwark against emergent black Africa. However, during the 1950s, the more pressing issue was that of the three High Commission Territories (HCTs).

Basutoland, Bechuanaland and Swaziland had not been incorporated into the Union of South Africa in 1910 but provision had been made for the possibility of their later transfer. Their geographical position, with Basutoland entirely surrounded, and

Bechuanaland and Swaziland bounded on three sides by South Africa, together with their acute dependence upon their white neighbour as its labour reserves and as members of a common monetary and customs union, made them extensions of the South African economy. The Nationalists regarded them as outposts of the empire, whose natural destiny lay with South Africa. There was also a desire to extend the Union's 'native policy' to the Protectorates, lest any advantages which their inhabitants might enjoy unsettle the Union's own Africans. Accordingly, successive Union governments sought to negotiate the transfer of the Protectorates to South Africa.

In the early 1950s, the indefinite continuation of British supervision of the HCTs seemed as unattractive as it seemed impracticable for states with such small populations and limited resources to assume politically sovereign status. Yet, while imperial thinking remained unclear, it was politically necessary to honour a longstanding promise that the territories would not be incorporated into the Union unless their inhabitants were consulted, and these had continuously been opposed to such incorporation. It was politically impracticable for any British government to transfer them while South Africa continued to implement apartheid.

More was at stake for Pretoria than simply extending direct control over these territories which, if independent, might perhaps offer a threat to security and stability. Incorporation of the HCTs would mean that instead of the 13,7 per cent area of land of the Union which the consolidated 'bantu' areas would comprise, 47 per cent of the enlarged South Africa would be reserved for Africans.[9] Apart from this, there was considerable concern about how developments within the HCTs might affect the government's policy of separate development. Although the bantustan strategy was premised upon the segregationist notion that Africans would develop along their own lines, the NP initially rejected opposition claims that their scheme implied political independence, and argued that the bantu areas would remain under white guardianship indefinitely. However, if the HCTs were themselves advanced to independence by the British, then the likelihood that the bantustans would remain incorporated within the Union would be reduced. And for the majority of white politicians at this time, whether government or opposition, the prospect of bantustan autonomy was synonymous with communist infiltration and subversion.

As the 1950s progressed, the worst fears of the South African government were realised, with the HCTs moving cautiously but steadily towards independence. In turn, the bantustan policy began to evolve in parallel, so that from 1959 government rhetoric became increasingly redolent of the language of self-determination and decolonisation. The ultimate aim was the eventual formation of a southern African 'commonwealth', corresponding to the area of the greater southern Africa, which would have come about had the HCTs been incorporated. In the meantime, efforts previously aimed at securing the incorporation of the HCTs were redirected at circumventing their forthcoming independence by entangling them within the web of dependence upon the South African economy.

The gaining of independence by 17, mostly French, colonies in 1960 highlighted the transformation of relations between governments throughout Africa. South Africa, under Prime Ministers Strydom and Verwoerd, attempted to adjust by proposing coexistence between black and white states founded upon mutual recognition of one another's rights. When Ghana became independent in 1957, trade relations were maintained despite Ghana's opposition to apartheid. As the wave of decolonisation gained momentum, South Africa was to find itself gradually excluded from almost all African, and many other international organisations. South Africa's meddling in the Congo crisis, when Pretoria lent covert succour to the secessionist Katanga regime, drew a sharp line between white and newly independent black Africa. The Sharpeville massacre on 21 March 1960, when police fired on unarmed demonstrators protesting against the pass laws, provoked further mass defiance that led to the banning of the ANC and PAC, and widened the divide further. The NP's subsequent declaration of a republic on 31 May 1961 thus seemed like an act of defiance, and when Verwoerd's consequent reapplication to join the Commonwealth as a republican state floundered upon mainly Afro-Asian criticism, the government was subsequently forced to make a virtue of political isolation.

Although there was a flight of capital after Sharpeville, the new Republic was far from being isolated economically. The consolidation of state capitalism and the rise of an Afrikaner business class was accompanied by more extensive links with metropolitan capital. Nonetheless, if there was concern within the expanding secondary sector that the government was paying too little attention to promoting trade links with newly independent black states, events had shown that 'political questions had primacy in Africa at this time'.[10] With the prospects for political coexistence blocked, South African energies were now to be redirected into expanding relations with black Africa in the economic sphere.

STATE PARTNERSHIP WITH TRANSNATIONAL CAPITAL 1961–1976: SOUTH AFRICA'S EMERGENCE AS A SUB-IMPERIAL POWER

During the 1960s, the South African economy experienced one of the highest growth rates in the western world. Underlying this was a threefold increase in gross domestic investment from R1 163 million in 1961 to R3 642 million in 1970, and a rapid growth in the manufacturing sector, whose contribution to the Gross Domestic Product (GDP) now exceeded that of mining and agriculture combined. South Africa became the industrial giant of the African continent. The economic boom which South Africa experienced during the 1960s was based upon low wages for black labour and high profits for capital. The acquiescence of the black workforce was secured through influx controls, the pass laws, restrictions on unionisation, denial of the right to strike, and the migratory and bantustan systems. For transnational corporations, the particular attraction was not merely that wage costs were low, but that South Africa also offered a political stability and ideological commitment to capitalism that did not generally pertain/apply to black Africa. As a result, the corporate gains were consistently high. Between 1961 and 1965, their general profit rate of between 15 and 20 per cent annually was twice as high as the world average, and profits continued to rank among the highest in the world, until the economy began to slow down in the mid-1970s.

Following the outflow of capital after Sharpeville, South African-based finance and national capital moved swiftly to invest in a wide range of spheres. This laid the basis for the growing interpenetration, not only of Afrikaner with 'English-speaking' capital, but of national with transnational capital, which flowed back into South Africa once the state had demonstrated its capacity to crush all effective black opposition. Between 1960 and 1970 South Africa's total foreign liabilities grew from R3 024 million to R5 818 million, while direct foreign investment increased from R1 819 million to R3 943 million. In the meantime, growing competition by transnational corporations to expand trade and investments in South Africa led to a continuing diversification of trading partners and foreign investment. While British companies still provided the largest share of the latter, and Britain remained South Africa's largest export market, transnational corporations from elsewhere, notably the United States and West Germany, increased their stake in the economy substantially.

These various developments underwrote increasing economic

and covert political collaboration with the apartheid state. Not only did multinationals work closely with South African parastatals, but the British government, in particular, became engaged in direct investment through its nationalised corporations, such as British Steel and British Leyland in the South African industry, especially in iron and steel, chemicals, oil refining and transport. Despite the adoption of a voluntary UN embargo on the sale of arms in 1963, the western powers continued to supply South Africa with sophisticated weaponry. As South Africa began to move towards self-sufficiency in the production of arms, an 'invisible' arms trade involving many governments, notably the United States and Britain, developed and enabled the South African government to build up the most powerful military force on the continent.

In the changing international division of labour, which involved *inter alia*, a shift of productive investment away from metropolitan to 'semi-peripheral' countries with lower wage costs, South Africa emerged as a 'sub-imperial' power. The major features of this sub-imperialism were

(i) the growing partnership between South African and transnational capital which was integrally related to the former's domination of neighbouring countries as the regional centre for investment, services, technology and industry;
(ii) control of the state apparatus by the growing Afrikaner bourgeoisie, not only to repress the black population but also to organise the accumulation of capital to strengthen the relative power and autonomy of the South African economy globally;
(iii) the development of the industrial base, not so much to meet the material needs of the masses, but to satisfy the demand of the white population;
(iv) the existence of a skewed market which, because of the severely limited purchasing power of blacks, who constituted some 70 per cent of the population, led to an accumulation of excess productive capacity in the manufacturing sphere and thus required outlets in the neighbouring territories for its capital and products.

SOUTH AFRICA'S OUTWARD POLICY

The most immediate manifestation of South Africa's sub-imperial role was its 'outward' policy: the systematic expansion of its relations with white-controlled and any black-ruled states that were prepared to swallow their distaste for apartheid in return for perceived material or political advantage.[11] The way forward on the 'Great North Road' was cleared by Verwoerd's renunciation in 1964 of the South African ambition to incorporate the HCTs. The acceptance of the need to treat them formally as sovereign equals signified South Africa's adjustment to decolonisation and eased the diplomatic recognition of other black African states. Yet, visions of 'co-prosperity' or of a southern African 'commonwealth' failed because of the unequal relation between an overbearing South Africa and economically dependent, but racially sensitive neighbouring states.

The outward movement had major political, diplomatic and military objectives. It also offered material gains for South African-based capital in the form of larger markets, expanding spheres for investment and the maintenance of the existing supply of foreign migrant labour. By deliberately maintaining a reserve army of employable labour, South African-based capital was able to minimise labour shortages and undercut wage demands by the black workforce. The largest employer of foreign labour was the Chamber of Mines, whose post-war recruitment structure was shaped, until the early 1970s, by the internationally fixed price of gold. This limited the capacity of the mining companies to transfer increases in wage costs to consumers, and perpetuated production methods that depended on the extensive use of unskilled, cheap labour. In contrast, the expanding secondary sector was able to pay somewhat higher wages, with the result that it drew domestic labour away from the mines, which became more dependent upon foreign sources. Whereas in 1946 some 56 per cent of the black workforce on the mines originated from outside South Africa, by the early 1970s the proportion had risen to about 75 per cent. Consequently, the maintenance of foreign supplies of workers from Angola, Botswana, Lesotho, Malawi, Mozambique and Swaziland became an important policy objective. After independence, Tanzania and Zambia banned the recruitment of their nationals for work in South Africa, and this indicated that decolonisation meant that historical sources of labour could no longer be taken for granted.

But cheap labour was not the only resource to be drawn from neighbouring countries. An increasing need for energy led the South African government to collaborate with Portuguese and transnational corporations in the building of hydroelectric projects such as Cahora Bassa in Mozambique and the Kunene River in Angola. Natural gas was piped from southern Mozambique to the southern Transvaal and negotiations were started, only to be broken off until the 1980s, for the construction of dams in Lesotho that would supply electricity and much-needed water to South Africa's industrial heartland. South African mining houses and transnational firms became increasingly engaged in the extraction of mineral wealth from neighbouring states. For instance, the Anglo-American Corporation partnered the Zambian government in the production of copper and, in the late 1970s, the Botswana government in the extraction of nickel and copper from its Selebi-Pikwe mine. But the major case of South African involvement in mineral extraction beyond its borders was in Namibia. Here multinational corporations and South African firms, notably De Beers Consolidated Diamond Mines, the Tsumeb Corporation and from the mid-1970s, Rio Tinto Zinc, plundered the country's wide variety of minerals; especially diamonds, copper and uranium.

Yet, the economic dimension most unambiguously associated with the outward policy was South Africa's urgent search for new markets. This was necessitated by two related factors. Firstly, throughout the 1960s, South Africa's high rate of economic growth was accompanied by serious balance of payments problems. Although imbalances on the current account were offset by regular surpluses on the capital account, the South African government looked to increase manufacturing exports through foreign investment to rectify what was a structurally unstable situation. Secondly, inherent limits were placed on the domestic consumer market by the low wages paid to the majority of the black population. Consequently, the secondary manufacturing sector, whose rapid growth was fuelled by large inflows of foreign funds, could avoid stagnation only by expanding exports both of goods and surplus capital. Although impoverished and underdeveloped, African countries offered a rapidly expanding and potentially lucrative market, which South Africa was geographically well placed to exploit.

The result was a determined push into Africa by the South African manufacturing sector. In 1960, the only state in Africa with which South Africa conducted a significant export trade was the Central African Federation, but by 1970 South Africa had displaced Britain as the main exporter to Rhodesia, and both as the main exporter to Zambia. New trade agreements were signed with Rhodesia and the Portuguese territories and in March 1967 with Malawi, the first with a black state. Meanwhile, the customs union which had bound the HCTs to South Africa since 1910 was replaced by a new agreement in 1969, which, while somewhat more advantageous to the three smaller countries, continued to bind them closely to the white economy and was protective of South African industry. Exports to a growing number of black African states, including Zaire, the Ivory Coast and Gabon were steadily increasing. Such goods were often being 'laundered' by reprocessing or repackaging in third party states, such as Mauritius.

Associated with South Africa's export drive was an attempt to divide the continent's opponents of apartheid by establishing cooperative relations with willing black African states. During the 1960s, when African states were still emerging from colonialism, opposition to apartheid and commitment to the liberation of southern Africa became an article of faith which found expression in the founding charter of the Organisation of African Unity (OAU). While it was readily admitted that independent Africa was too weak to challenge South Africa economically and militarily, even a collection of weak states could, through united action, serve as an international pressure group for isolating the apartheid regime.

Yet, this was a fragile unity and was not to last for long. The transition to independence of Zambia, Malawi, Lesotho, Botswana and Swaziland, all of which exhibited varying degrees of dependence upon South Africa rendered impractical any total boycott of South Africa. Conservative leaders such as Chief Leabua Jonathan and President Hastings Banda were opposed to total boycott. Ironically, attempts to impose sanctions against Rhodesia after Ian Smith's Unilateral Declaration of Independence (UDI) in 1965 made Zambia, in particular, more rather than less dependent on South Africa. Furthermore, African states failed to take a united line against British reluctance to act decisively against UDI and were unable to intervene militarily against Rhodesia or to support adequately the first guerrilla forays, which were of limited impact. This served to undermine the prospects of success for any radical strategy premised upon bringing about change in South Africa through diplomatic isolation and external pressure.

The OAU's advocacy of a trade boycott of South Africa represented a counter to South Africa's outward thrust. But South Africa's objectives were more than economic, and accompanying its exports were promises of aid. The government reduced its rather limited contributions to international schemes by providing instead for the direct channelling of low-interest loans to African countries in forms which could be clearly identified as South African. The amount of this aid was not large, but was concentrated in a few countries. In 1972, for instance, the total extent of financial assistance of R171 million was dispensed to Malawi, Madagascar, Swaziland, Lesotho and Mozambique for the creation of infrastructural projects which would integrate regional economies into the South African network.

South Africa's greatest successes were with Malawi and Madagascar. The former was to become its foremost ally in black Africa, becoming the first independent African state to exchange diplomatic representation with Pretoria in 1967. This was later followed by a visit in May 1970 of Prime Minister Vorster to Malawi; a return tour of South Africa by Banda in 1971; and the acceptance of a South African military attache in Blantyre. President Banda maintained that Malawi's foreign policy was dictated by the realities of its poverty, dependency and its geographical position. However, a more likely rationale lay in the benefits of South African collaboration in securing him against his domestic opponents who had fled the country in the early 1960s.[12] Meanwhile, South Africa's relations with Madagascar were built upon the conservative Tsirana government's desire to liberate itself from French economic and cultural domination, while simultaneously strengthening its defences against perceived Chinese and Russian threats to Indian Ocean and domestic security.

French foreign policy involved closer collaboration with Pretoria. This entailed a total disregard for the 1963 UN embargo on the sale of arms. However, despite increasing criticism from Africa, it was not uncommon for francophone states seeking to increase their standing with France to adopt a conciliatory position towards South Africa, especially if this was consistent with their own conservatism. This was the case with President Houpouët-Boigny of the Ivory Coast, who in November 1970 declared the failure of existing strategies against apartheid and called for an African conference to discuss an alternative of dialogue. The Ivory Coast had no apparent economic motive for leading the dialogue campaign, and it is likely that Houpouët-Boigny took up the issue on account of his close ties with Tsirana. However, the timing of his call was probably influenced by the campaign being waged by the OAU and Non-Aligned Movement (NAM) to block the newly elected Conservative government of Edward Heath in Britain from resuming the sale of arms to South Africa.

The idea of dialogue was concomitant with the position adopted in April 1969 by the heads of state and government in east and central Africa in the 'Lusaka Manifesto'. This manifesto registered something of a retreat from the OAU's uncompromising stand towards South Africa, emphasising a preference for conciliation and non-violent change, yet calling for the boycotting and isolation of South Africa if it showed no signs of abandoning apartheid. Nonetheless, the notion of promoting dialogue received considerable support from francophone Africa, including the Central African Republic, Gabon, Dahomey, Togo and Niger, while being roundly rejected by others, notably Guinea, Senegal and the Cameroon. Meanwhile, in anglophone Africa, although Kenya and Sierra Leone vacillated before finally opposing dialogue, Houpouët-Boigny found three of his most vocal supporters in Ghana, Lesotho and Malawi. Yet, such support was compromised. Kofi Busia, Prime Minister of Ghana, was a known conservative; Leabua Jonathan's government in Lesotho had been kept in power by covert South African support in a disputed election earlier in 1970; and Banda had already forged his connection with the apartheid regime.

The attempts by Houpouët-Boigny to have dialogue discussed by the OAU summit in 1971 were defeated. Instead, leaders of east and central African states soon moved beyond the Lusaka Manifesto to adopt a Mogadishu Declaration which endorsed armed struggle as the sole way of achieving liberation in southern Africa and condemned African states who wanted to maintain closer links with apartheid South Africa. Although the Ivory Coast, Malawi and Lesotho sought to keep it alive, the removal by the military of both the Busia and Tsirana regimes in their respective countries was to rob dialogue of two of its leading supporters. Soon thereafter, even Leabua Jonathan, dissatisfied with the amount of South African aid, realised the need to reconcile the Lesotho citizens with his government's disputed rule. He began to adopt an increasingly radical posture, which soon paid dividends in facilitating a flow of economic assistance from elsewhere and by increasing Lesotho's international stature.

While South Africa was seeking friends in black Africa, it was simultaneously consolidating ties with neighbouring white regimes. Portuguese resistance to decolonisation was welcomed in Pretoria, because Angola and Mozambique were located strategically as buffer states. In addition, given the flow of labour from both countries to South African mines, especially from Mozambique, together with the potential market they offered when much of Africa remained closed, there were sound economic, as well as military reasons for strengthening collaboration. Although South African trade with Angola and Mozambique during the 1960s was not very substantial, this was destined to grow significantly, the balance of trade lying very markedly in South Africa's favour.

The Portuguese, claiming their colonies to be overseas extensions of the metropolis, were reluctant to isolate themselves from the international community. Accordingly, they attempted to divorce themselves from apartheid, which they argued compared unfavourably with their own policy of Lusitanian assimilation. But political distance between Pretoria and Lisbon became narrower as the colonial regime came under increasing pressure, notably from the nationalist guerrillas who waged a protracted struggle for liberation from 1961 in Angola and 1964 in Mozambique. Thereafter, the Portuguese sought to resist decolonisation by encouraging the large-scale migration of white settlers from the motherland, and by opening up the territories to foreign investment. Hence it was that South African capital flowed freely into both Angola and Mozambique. The Portuguese objective of basing colonial development on mineral and resource extraction was concomitant with South Africa's own industrial needs. Although the search for oil in Angola was dominated by Portuguese concerns, and the Portuguese were successful in attracting international investment from the United States, Britain and Europe to assist in financing their various schemes, such ventures as Cahora Bassa, the Kunene River project and the construction of the natural gas pipeline from Mozambique to the Transvaal would not have been possible without South African finance, expertise and, most critically, guarantee of a future market.

As the guerrilla threat increased, with the Frente de Libertação de Moçambique (Frelimo) in particular being determined to halt the construction of the Cahora Bassa Dam, South Africa became more closely involved in the defence of the Portuguese empire. However, the bulk of such assistance lay in the provision of supplies and extensive exchange in intelligence rather than in direct military involvement. South Africa was as wary of becoming engaged in an expensive, extended encounter as Portugal was cautious about encouraging the growth of South African influence in the determination of its colonial future. Yet, even if political tensions overlaid a more fundamental imperialist harmony, South Africa remained sensitive to Portuguese aspirations. This was because friendship with Portugal was seen as an entry into South America as South Africa's outward policy soon stretched beyond Africa to involve the forging of bilateral economic and military links with a number of regimes in South America.

DÉTENTE: PHASE ONE

The UDI of Ian Smith in November 1965 clarified South Africa's sub-imperial role: it was compromised by South Africa's outward thrust and the forging of closer bonds with Lisbon, Salisbury and Pretoria. It introduced an enormously complicating factor into South Africa's external relations, yet in the absence of an independence settlement, which would have effectively legitimised white rule, Pretoria's support was guaranteed by its need to keep decolonisation at bay.

Without South African and Portuguese assistance, Rhodesia would have been denied oil, transport links and vital supplies. Yet South African commitment was not unambiguous because it eschewed recognition of the illegal regime and espoused a formal neutrality, which urged a negotiated settlement between the British and the Rhodesian governments. South African efforts were devoted to ensuring that British-imposed and UN-mandated sanctions against Rhodesia were rendered ineffective, in part to discourage the adoption of such a weapon against South Africa. And when British determination to end the rebellion proved irresolute, the South African government did not hesitate in 1967 to send its police to assist the Rhodesian military confront insurgents on the grounds that South African ANC guerrillas were fighting alongside the Zimbabwe African People's Union (ZAPU).

Confidence in the enduring strength of the white entente encouraged Vorster, who had succeeded Verwoerd as prime minister in 1966, in promoting dialogue. Yet, as long as South Africa succeeded in supporting only known conservative states, prospects for securing a major breakthrough into black Africa remained non-existent. Hence, from 1968 the South African government engaged in secret contacts with Zambia, the black state in southern Africa most openly identified with opposition to the various white regimes.

Before independence, President Kenneth Kaunda had been closely aligned with the nationalist movements opposing minority rule in Rhodesia, colonialism in Angola and Mozambique, and apartheid in South Africa. Yet, Zambia's dependence upon South

Africa – notably the domination of its copper-mining industry by the Anglo-American Corporation and its reliance upon South Africa for skilled human resources, transport routes and imports – imposed the necessity of economic links with the apartheid state. Nonetheless, the Zambian government sought to disengage from South Africa by extending its transport networks and trade with black Africa, while simultaneously offering nationalist guerrillas substantial material and political support.

Although South Africa's collaboration with Rhodesia and Portugal intensified hostility across the Zambezi, its policy towards Zambia remained one of restraint. Zambia symbolised the great prize whose capture would crown the outward movement with lasting success. The South African government realised that the abandoning of the pan-African strategy by the Kaunda regime would deprive nationalist guerrillas of their land base and undermine the perceived credibility of the militant armed struggle against white rule in favour of more gradualist compromise founded upon 'economic realism'. For his part, Kaunda did not repudiate the South African government's covert initiatives, reasoning that he might thereby dissuade Vorster from lending the Rhodesian regime its unequivocal assistance.

Kaunda's role in promulgating the Lusaka Manifesto of 1969 was consistent with his objective of avoiding a confrontation with South Africa. If it did little to endear him to Pretoria, his explicitly non-Marxist ideology of humanism and his accommodation to transnational firms at home marked him as a political moderate with whom South Africa could have relations. However, his accession to the chairmanship of the OAU in 1970, and his resulting prominence in campaigns against dialogue and the resumption by Britain of its arms sales to South Africa, were to render him an obstacle to the apartheid regime's immediate goals. Consequently, Vorster attempted to expose Kaunda as duplicitous by revealing secret correspondence with him. However, Vorster's breach of confidence brought condemnation even from his partners in dialogue, who were afraid of being exposed as being involved with South Africa. And if his revelations were intended to precipitate Kaunda's overthrow by his domestic opponents, they failed, even though they succeeded in highlighting the ambiguities which Zambia's dependence imposed upon its foreign policy.

South Africa's concern with the mounting guerrilla threat in Angola and Mozambique, together with a major strike by workers and increased activity by the South West African People's

Organisation (SWAPO) in Namibia, led to more extensive collaboration with Portugal. A breakthrough by the Zimbabwean guerrillas from 1971 onwards also led to a greater South African involvement in counter-insurgency alongside Rhodesian security forces. Consequently, South African relations with Zambia continued to deteriorate, with Pretoria voicing particular concern at the strategic implications of the Chinese built Tan-Zam railway, which gave Zambia access to the sea, and expressing 'mounting impatience' with the operation of 'terrorists' from Zambia.

The South African government's support of Rhodesia was not without its strains. A case in point was Vorster's anger towards Ian Smith's unilateral closing of his border with Zambia in January 1973 in retaliation for that country's harbouring of guerrillas. Kaunda's response of making the closure permanent reinforced the South African conviction that air strikes on the guerrilla camps in Zambia would have been more propitious than a move which encouraged economic disengagement. Even so, for all the difficulties, Pretoria's continuing support for the illegal regime was premised upon the determination to keep the guerrilla threat away from South Africa's own borders.

The *coup d'etat* of 25 April 1974 in which the Portuguese armed forces, disillusioned and radicalised by the colonial wars, overthrew the authoritarian state, transformed regional relations. The new military government was divided between the revolutionary left, which argued for independence for the African colonies, and the supporters of the new president, General Spinola, who favoured an explicitly neo-colonial Lusitanian federation of the metropole with self-governing colonies. In spite of this, it was clear that the alliance between South Africa, Portugal and Rhodesia had been breached irrevocably. Rhodesia and Namibia could expect to become exposed to guerrilla pressure from the Portuguese borders that once protected them. South Africa had to reckon with a re-evaluation in western capitals of their policies, which had been based on the mistaken assumption of the invulnerability of white power.

The South African government gave immediate recognition to the new Portuguese authorities and indicated that it would cooperate with the government in Mozambique, led by the self-proclaimed Marxist-Leninist Frelimo, which it now perceived as inevitably coming to power. Acceptance of a liberated Mozambique was based not merely on optimism concerning the extent of that country's economic dependence upon South Africa, but also upon the need to secure a continuation of the flow of Mozambican workers to the mines and the supply of energy from Cahora Bassa. The South African government also wanted to obtain a guarantee that Mozambican territory would not be used as a base for guerrilla attacks in South African territory. Accordingly, there was no South African support for an attempted putsch by rightwing settlers in Lourenço Marques, renamed Maputo, in September 1974. This was rewarded by a reciprocally pragmatic orientation towards South Africa by the incoming Frelimo government. Importantly, however, Frelimo made the withdrawal of South African forces from Rhodesia a precondition of all future negotiation.

This brought a fundamental reassessment of South Africa's foreign policy towards Rhodesia. Minority rule in that country was now seen as doomed, and it became the South African goal to avoid extensive military involvement alongside Rhodesian security in an intensifying war which would become increasingly costly and which would isolate South Africa even more internationally. Regional stability, required for the preservation of the apartheid political economy, was now defined and cited to convince the Smith regime of its fateful destiny and ease the transition to a moderate black government in Rhodesia which would restore peace internally, receive recognition internationally and co-operate functionally with South Africa. However the constraints of white politics in South Africa meant that Vorster could not ditch Smith too unceremoniously, and the only way in which his government could secure its new objectives was through bringing about a negotiated settlement between the contending forces.

It was the essence of the ensuing period of détente that this aim coincided with some of the interests of South Africa's black neighbours. In the case of Zambia, whose economy was confronted by a drastic decline in the government's economic management, elements within the governing class saw détente leading to an inflow of foreign investment and commodities, thereby alleviating the immediate crisis. Furthermore the ruling elements of the other Front Lines States (FLS) – Botswana, Tanzania, Mozambique and Angola – whose economies were also ailing, were eager to achieve some measure of political accommodation. Consequently, the basis of the deal was that while Vorster would deliver Smith to the conference table to negotiate majority rule, the FLS would ensure the co-operation of the Zimbabwean liberation movements.

The substantive result of détente was the Lusaka Agreement of December 1974. This agreement was made possible by Vorster leaning upon Smith to secure the release of the nationalist leadership which had been imprisoned before UDI. This included Joshua Nkomo, President of ZAPU, and Robert Mugabe and Ndabaningi Sithole of ZANU. The agreement was further facilitated by FLS Presidents, Kaunda, Nyerere and Botswana's Seretse Khama. They bludgeoned the nationalist movements ZANU, ZAPU and the smaller FROLIZI into uniting under the rubric of the African Nationalist Council, headed by Bishop Abel Muzorewa, to negotiate a settlement with Smith.

The Lusaka Agreement resulted in a ceasefire as a preliminary to constitutional negotiations. However, there were disagreements about the terms of the truce. For their part, the nationalist leaders claimed that they would only agree to suspend the armed struggle once Smith had agreed to a number of preconditions, including the release of political prisoners, the lifting of bans on ZANU and ZAPU and the permitting of free political activity. The Rhodesian premier announced that he had received a guarantee that 'terrorist' activity in Rhodesia would cease with immediate effect and the proposed constitutional conference would take place without 'preconditions'.[13] Consequently, although something of a ceasefire came into effect on 11 December 1974, conflicting interpretations by both sides about what had been agreed upon led to a resumption of hostilities the next month.

With détente in danger of collapse, the FLS presidents and Vorster sought to cajole their respective allies back to the negotiating table. The constitutional conference agreed upon was convened on 25 August 1975 on a train parked on the Victoria Falls Bridge between Rhodesia and Zambia. To reach this stage, however, Vorster had had to exert pressure upon the minority regime to the extent of withdrawing all South African forces from Rhodesia, while the FLS had sought to contain opposition to détente within the nationalist movements. Joshua Nkomo of ZAPU emerged as the one leader who combined the virtues of widespread legitimacy, eagerness to negotiate a settlement, and was acceptable to Vorster as the potential head of a 'moderate' majority-rule regime. Kenneth Kaunda moved to suppress ZANU within his territory, while Tanzanian and Mozambican troops took over guerrilla camps in their own countries and restricted the flow of weapons to ZANU. But with the nationalists locked together in only an externally imposed unity, and with Smith determined not to give way, the talks were doomed to an early demise, despite the active personal interventions of both Kaunda and Vorster. However, Nkomo pursued talks with Smith independently of the other nationalist factions, lasting from December 1975 through to March 1976. But South Africa was preoccupied with the outbreak of the Angolan civil war, and these negotiations failed, not merely upon Smith's continuing intransigence, but also as a result of the reassessment of their objectives and strategies by the backers of the détente exercise.

At the time of the April 1974 coup, the Portuguese retained a favourable position in Angola, where the nationalist forces were divided between three competing parties: the Movimento Popular de Libertação de Angola (MPLA), whose support was located principally in the Luanda area and which enjoyed the backing of the Soviet Union; the Frente Naçional de Libertação de Angola (FNLA), representative mainly of ethnic Bakongo and supported by the United States-backed Mobuto regime in Zaire; and Uniao Nacional para a Independencia Total de Angola (Unita), the smallest of the three groups, led by Jonas Savimbi, and based in Zambia and eastern Zaire. The Portuguese decolonisation strategy was based on the Alvar Agreement of January 1975, which had included Unita at the last moment in a bid to balance the two older parties, and scheduled independence for 11 November 1975. The various parties agreed to remain within their own liberated areas; to co-operate in the building of a national army; and to participate in a transitional government which would draw up a constitution and allow for elections before independence.

Angola was the most valuable of Portugal's African territories. By 1974, it was the third largest oil-producing country on the continent, as well as a significant source of coffee, diamonds and other minerals including iron ore, copper and uranium. When the Alvar Agreement collapsed in March 1975, as the FNLA strove to drive the MPLA out of its Luanda base, the conflict rapidly became internationalised. The Portuguese army was divided and demoralised to the extent that its major concern was to extricate itself from the country. Congo-Brazzaville and Zaire favoured the MPLA and FNLA respectively and both eyed the oil-producing Cabinda enclave jealously, while the major Western powers and South Africa gave their clandestine backing to FNLA and Unita. But as the MPLA mobilised its support in Luanda and rapidly took the offensive, threatening to establish control over most of the country by the date set for independence, western assistance to their clients became more overt in the form of finance, weapons and mercenaries. However, on the understanding that it would receive United States' support, the South African government sent between 2 000 and 3 000 troops across the border to confront the MPLA.

The South African Defence Force (SADF) enjoyed rapid, early success, penetrating far into Angola, but it soon encountered two obstacles that were fatal to its desire for a quick campaign and which would leave the western-backed FNLA and Unita in power. Firstly, the MPLA received substantial military assistance in the form of large supplies of weapons from the Soviet Union and up to 9 000 troops from Cuba. Secondly, fearing it would be embroiled in a second Vietnam, the United States congress declined to support plans for more extensive involvement in the conflict. Despite desperate attempts by some western interests and various African leaders, notably Kaunda, to secure the formation of a new coalition government, the Cuban-backed MPLA pressed on to victory over its rivals sufficient to gain diplomatic recognition from most African states, which were outraged by the South African invasion. The MPLA was acknowledged as the legitimate government of Angola in February 1976. South African troops were forced to beat a humiliating retreat in exchange for an MPLA guarantee of the security of the hydroelectric Kunene Dam.

The South African invasion had been launched in the name of détente, to which a victory of the MPLA was fatal. Indeed, it is probable that the South African action had the covert blessing of both the Zambian and Zairean governments which supported Unita and FNLA respectively, both preferring to see a pro-western, non-radical government assuming power in Luanda. But as continental anger at the South African government crystallised, no African leader could afford to be associated with the aggressive intentions of the apartheid regime. Even worse, from the South African viewpoint, was the fact that the Angolan war now shifted the initiative to the radicals among the FLS, who now favoured a resumption of the armed struggle in Rhodesia. Détente was not yet dead, but it was only with considerable difficulty that it could be revived.

THE CRISIS OF THE APARTHEID STATE: FROM DÉTENTE TO DESTABILISATION

Détente, which had been laid to rest by the Angolan debacle, had specific political objectives, notably an end to war and a negotiated transition in Zimbabwe. It also had an economic basis in the asymmetric relation between South Africa's expansionism and black Africa's dependence. Between 1966 and 1976, South African exports to other parts of Africa rose by R256 million to R453 million, an increase of 130 per cent. Imports rose by R181 million to R310 million, an increase of 141 per cent, giving a healthy balance of trade surplus in South Africa's favour. Nonetheless, South Africa's outward thrust was encountering serious limitations. The proportion of South African exports going to the rest of Africa was subject to a dramatic decline. While 19 per cent of South African exports went to Africa in 1964, and remained at this level until 1971, the proportion dropped to 10 per cent by 1980. This seems not to have been a result of the supposed OAU boycott on South Africa goods, for by 1981 South Africa claimed to be doing business, directly or indirectly, with 47 of Africa's 51 independent states. However, it did imply the need and scope for further economic penetration if South Africa was to maximise the economic benefits of its location. As it was, the proportionate decline in South African exports to Africa was a contributory factor to the slump that afflicted its manufacturing sector during the mid-1970s.

Equally important was the major shift in trading and investment relations on the part of western countries towards black Africa and away from South Africa. Thus, whereas new investments and reinvested earnings by the US firms amounted to $9 million and $73 million respectively in 1976, the comparable figures for Africa as a whole were $256 million and $4 584 million. Similarly, while South Africa was Britain's third largest export market in 1967, buying 5 per cent of all British merchandise exports, it had fallen to sixteenth in 1977, taking only 1,8 per cent of such exports. In contrast, by 1978 Nigeria had become Britain's ninth largest trading partner and, having surpassed South Africa in total trade with the US in 1973, supplied 16 per cent of US oil imports in 1980. But what gave Nigeria its particular importance in the southern African context in the late 1970s was its declared intention to use its newly acquired leverage to cajole the West into extracting concessions from white minority regimes in Africa.

DÉTENTE: PHASE TWO

The Cuban engagement in Angola had given cause for the US under the Republican administration of Gerald Ford to award greater priority to southern Africa in order to contain 'Soviet expansionism'. Accordingly, it was signalled to Pretoria that in return for South Africa's agreeing to cajole Smith into conceding a negotiated settlement, the US would use its influence to divert international pressure away from South Africa. Despite the rift over Angola, spurred by the explosion of Soweto on 16 June 1976, Pretoria exerted the required force upon the Smith government, which on 24 September 1976 announced its willingness to negotiate a transition to majority rule within two years. However, the subsequent October–December 1976 constitutional conference in Geneva collapsed when it became clear that the ruling Rhodesian Front was not prepared to confer more than an appearance of political power on the African majority, and was determined to retain effective control over both the government and the economy.

When the Democratic administration of Jimmy Carter assumed office in 1977 it initiated a sweeping reassessment of US foreign policy. As far as Africa was concerned, this involved a recognition of expanding US material interest in black Africa, especially Nigeria, while Carter's 'human rights' stance also resulted in a more open critique of apartheid. Furthermore, the US gave its support to the mandatory arms embargo imposed by the UN after the South African regime cracked down on black militants when it banned 34 political organisations in October 1977. The subsequent deterioration of relations between Washington and Pretoria resulted in a major South African policy shift in favour of Ian Smith's efforts to find an 'internal settlement'. Propelled by the urgency of a marked escalation of the liberation war, notably by ZANU, and with victory becoming increasingly unlikely, the Ian Smith regime was now engaged in feverish efforts to manipulate divisions within nationalist ranks in order to forge a working alliance with 'moderate' black leaders. Initially, Smith sought to come to an agreement with Nkomo, seen as a Kenyatta-like pro-capitalist leader. However, when this failed, Smith turned to Abel Muzorewa, now leader of the United African Nationalist Council (UANC), and they reached an agreement on the 3 March 1978.

This internal settlement made provision for a majority rule constitution, but involved the preservation of white seats in parliament, a white veto over further constitutional change for ten years, and effective white control over the military, internal security, the civil service and the judiciary. It also guaranteed existing rights of property, pensions and public employment. Furthermore, although Muzorewa assumed office as prime minister of Zimbabwe-Rhodesia after his UANC won 51 out of 72 African seats in the April 1979 election, his government embraced a coalition with the Rhodesian Front, and the substance of power still remained with Ian Smith.

The internal settlement was condemned by the UN, the OAU and both wings of the PF, which stepped up their guerrilla campaign, ZANU operating from Mozambique and ZAPU from Zambia. Although failure to end the war led to a steady erosion of Muzorewa's domestic support, South African material and military backing was vital in enabling the Zimbawe-Rhodesian regime to survive. Pretoria viewed Muzorewa's government as viable, for the prospects of Muzorewa gaining international recognition seemed to have become more propitious. Zambia, undergoing the throes of an acute foreign exchange crisis, had reopened the border with Rhodesia in October 1978 to clear a backlog of copper exports and was desperate for a settlement, as was Mozambique whose territory was continuously being violated by Rhodesian air strikes and military raids. Pretoria's relations with Washington were steadily thawing as the Carter administration became increasingly concerned with the Soviet penetration of Africa and the Cuban troops being used in Ethiopia as well as in Angola. Furthermore, in May 1979, a Conservative government under Margaret Thatcher swept to power in Britain and seemed set to recognise the Muzorewa regime.

But such recognition never materialised. In addition, Nigeria linked its nationalisation of British Petroleum, its refusal to countenance British firms' bids for federal contracts, and other economic measures to British plans for legitimising the internal settlement. Apart from Britain, the United States was warned of the costs which a commitment to Muzorewa would entail. As a result, previous Anglo-American proposals for a settlement that included the PF were revived, culminating in the convening of the Lancaster House conference in December 1979. With the West and South Africa pressurising Smith and Muzorewa, and with the FLS levering both ZAPU and ZANU, which were reluctant to make compromising concessions, agreement was reached on new elections and a settlement.

The subsequent victory of Robert Mugabe's ZANU, which in the March 1980 elections won 51 out of 80 seats in a 100-seat parliament, shattered British calculations, which had been based upon an assumption that no one party could secure an absolute majority. The British were of the opinion that that ZANU, whose explicitly socialist programme was viewed as a severe threat to western interests, would be excluded from power, hopefully through a coalition between UANC, ZAPU and even the Rhodesian Front. But the government that took power was effectively run by ZANU, although Joshua Nkomo and ZAPU were incorporated into a coalition as subordinates.

RESPONSE TO CRISIS: SOUTH AFRICA'S TOTAL STRATEGY IN SOUTHERN AFRICA

South Africa's acceptance of the Lancaster House conference had been premised on the expectation of a Muzorewa victory at the polls or the election of a 'moderate' coalition government, which the FLS would be forced to recognise by their vested interests in the settlement. But South African confidence that Muzorewa enjoyed greater domestic support than the 'terrorists' was wrong, and Mugabe's victory was received in Pretoria with a profound sense of shock. Nonetheless, Prime Minister PW Botha, who had succeeded Vorster in 1978, resisted the temptation to support a post-electoral coup by Rhodesian security forces and thereafter announced a policy of neutrality. Although the Mugabe regime was regarded with considerable misgivings, solace was found in the new Zimbabwean government's initial strenuous efforts to forge national reconciliation between blacks and whites, the moderation of its socialist programme, and its declared intention of courting foreign investment. Mugabe's immediate post-independence need for coexistence with South Africa was therefore cautiously reciprocated.

South Africa's ties with other neighbouring states mirrored the confirmation of these links with Zimbabwe. Mozambique, for example, continued to supply migrant workers to the mines, while South Africa made considerable use of Mozambican railways and harbours, and continued to receive electrical power from the Cahora Bassa Dam. Meanwhile, Zambia increased both its imports and exports with South Africa. However, the settlement in Zimbabwe meant that South Africa was more isolated than ever before. Although the immediate attentions of the international community were directed at the securing of an independence settlement for Namibia, no one could doubt that this would form but a prelude to an increasingly determined assault upon the apartheid regime itself.

The response of the regime was both proactive and pre-emptive. Under Botha, it became articulated in 'total strategy', a response to a perceived communist-inspired 'total onslaught', which manifested itself in the growth of black militancy both internally as well externally. Total strategy constituted 'both the consolidation of a new dominant alliance between monopoly capital and the military within the state, and the *reorganisation of the ruling capitalist class* to deal with this crisis'.[14] Although this was to see the rise to dominance of security interests within the state, with the subordination of the cabinet and parliament to the overarching control of the State Security Council, total strategy was much more than a militarist initiative. Its key proponents repeatedly stressed that the survival of the apartheid state depended primarily upon an adequate political response to the crises that the regime was facing both internally and externally.

The restructuring of the apartheid state precipitated open fissure within the white ruling bloc. This was signified most immediately by the breakaway in 1981 of right-wing elements, led by former cabinet minister Andries Treurnicht, who were unable to stomach political and economic measures which were intended to reduce internal pressures upon the regime. These included the absorption of key segments of the coloured and Indian populations into the central polity via a tripartite parliamentary structure ultimately controlled by whites, and the attempted co-option of the urban African population by easing access to residence rights, home ownership, education and labour rights. However, total strategy, presented as 'reform', enjoyed the initial enthusiastic backing of the US, where Ronald Reagan had succeeded Jimmy Carter as president in 1980, and Britain, as well as the domestic and international business community. Outside the country, total strategy was implemented in four stages.[15]

(i) The constellation of states initiative

In November 1979 Botha voiced his intention to establish a 'constellation of states', an initiative which though never systematically spelt out revived the Verwoerdian aspirations for the formalisation of South African hegemony. It operated at three levels. First of all, there was an economic thrust, with Botha calling for support from the private sector for a proposed Southern African Development Bank which would finance infrastructural projects and provide a framework for regional growth and development. This would serve to attract co-operation from neighbouring countries; and would provide a platform for increasing the exports of both South African capital and goods. Secondly, there was a major political objective. Pretoria reckoned that if Zimbabwe could gain its independence under Muzorewa, then Malawi and Swaziland, both extremely conservative states which already had strong economic links with South Africa, could be drawn into formal regional co-operation. This would leave little option for Botswana and Lesotho, the other two members of the customs union, to join with the possibility that Zaire and Zambia could then be induced to affiliate. Namibia, which apartheid strategists were by now hoping to bring to a Muzorewa-type internal settlement, would also join the club, leaving the other FLS – Angola, Mozambique and Tanzania – weak and isolated. Thirdly, having drawn neighbouring territories into a web of economic collaboration and dependence, Pretoria's intent was to forge links between an inner constellation of those bantustans which had accepted 'independence', namely the Transkei in 1976; Bophuthatswana in 1977; Venda in 1979; and Ciskei in 1981.

Botha's aspirations were thwarted by two developments. The first was the defeat of Muzorewa at the polls. Instead of becoming the foundation of the constellation, Zimbabwe became a member of the FLS. Secondly, the constellation idea was countered in April 1960 by the establishment of the Southern African Development Co-ordination Conference (SADCC), which drew all nine independent states in the region together in a joint developmental endeavour whose key objective was to bring about a reduction of their economic dependence upon South Africa. This represented a major defeat for the South African regional strategy, with the result that the constellation initiative was reduced to the institutions and relationships which described South Africa's links with the so-called 'TBVC' states.

(ii) The turn to destabilisation

Pretoria considered the fall of white power in Rhodesia as having brought the barbarians to South Africa's gate. Having failed to remould regional relations in a manner which would underpin South African hegemony, the apartheid regime turned to the much more aggressive strategy of destabilisation. Its objective was to undermine by both military and economic means the viability of any regional governments that chose to give support to the liberation movements, especially the ANC, SWAPO and their guerrillas.

Davies and O'Meara argue that this second phase of total strategy, which entailed the launch of destabilisation tactics 'in a fairly generalised and indiscriminate manner', lasted from mid-1980 to the end of 1981. It involved an increase in military action against neighbouring states. Thus, South Africa continued to lend substantial support to Unita in Angola, with the SADF making a number of major incursions into that country. The South African commandos made an assault upon an ANC base at Matola near Maputo in January 1981, and active support was extended to the Resistancia Nacional Mocambicana (Renamo), the anti-Frelimo group initially created by Rhodesian security forces. Assistance was also extended to the Lesotho Liberation Army (LLA), the military wing of the opposition Basutoland Congress Party, and direct actions, including assassinations, were taken against ANC personnel in a number of different countries. Secondly, South Africa turned to techniques of economic coercion to produce compliance. For instance, when Zimbabwe removed a number of privileges offered to South African as opposed to other foreign investors, South Africa responded with the withdrawal of 20 locomotives on hire to the National Railways of Zimbabwe at a time when they were in acute demand following a bumper maize harvest and the reopening of export routes following the ending of sanctions. Similar actions were taken against Mozambique, all in the cause of despatching the message that any attempts by neighbouring countries to sever their economic ties with South Africa would face extreme retaliation.

(iii) Intensified and selective destabilisation

From the beginning of 1982, destabilisation became more focussed and more intensive. In particular, two objectives were singled out. Firstly, actions were launched against neighbouring states, which were designed to force them to withdraw their support of the ANC and to impose constraints upon the ANC's capacity to go on waging the armed struggle. Secondly, the regime was determined to tighten economic links and to frustrate the mounting efforts by regional states to reduce their dependence upon South Africa. Davies and O'Meara argue that apartheid strategists divided states in the region into three categories in their application of their destabilisation tactics. Firstly, there were conservative states, which were seen as active or potential collaborators; secondly, there were uncooperative states which were vulnerable to pressure; and thirdly, there were those states whose political systems and development strategies were viewed as offering a fundamental challenge to apartheid capitalism.

States in the first category were offered inducements which would tighten their links to South Africa or rewards for good behaviour. Davies and O'Meara cite Swaziland as the most striking example: it received assistance to build a railway line through its territory linking the Eastern Transvaal with Richards Bay, and a supplementary R50 million payment via the SACU. Having offered to cede the KaNgwane bantustan and part of Kwazulu to Swaziland, an offer which had to be withdrawn when it ran into opposition at home, the South African government induced Swaziland into signing a secret non-aggression pact in February 1982, whose existence only became known two years later. This resulted in a severe clamp down on members of the ANC in Swaziland, which also diverted its sugar and other exports from Maputo to Richards Bay via the new railway line.

Lesotho and Zimbabwe constituted states in the second category, whose uncooperative behaviour was deemed by Pretoria as amenable to increased pressure. The LLA's armed campaign against Leabua Jonathan's regime opened with a series of attacks upon security personnel and government facilities in mid-1979, leading to allegations by Lesotho that South Africa was directly backing the rebels. Further attacks were made in 1980, but their intensity was reduced after a meeting between Chief Jonathan and South African Foreign Minister PW Botha on the border between the two countries in August of that year. But LLA attacks, which were largely launched from the Qwa-Qwa and Transkei bantustans adjoining Lesotho, were intensified again from mid-1981. During that year attacks took place largely in the Maseru area and seemed designed to target the tourist industry and government ministers. From the second half of 1982, the LLA turned its attentions more directly to attacking the Basotho state and its security forces, and seemed to have acquired greater capacity to engage in conventional military operations. Overall, there were at least 25 separate attacks by the LLA during 1981–82, including an attempt in July 1982 to assassinate Jonathan himself.[16]

With relations between the two countries having deteriorated, the SADF launched a bloody raid upon what it proclaimed to be ANC houses in Maseru in December 1982. During this attack 43 people were killed, many of them Lesotho nationals, including women and children. The SADF alleged that the ANC had been planning a series of attacks on South Africa from Lesotho. As Lesotho proceeded to extend its diplomatic ties with both the

Soviet Union and China, South Africa tightened the economic screws, and in May 1983, it imposed restrictions upon the movement of goods across the border and issued threats about repatriating Basotho migrant workers from South African mines. Eventually, Lesotho succumbed, and in June 1983, it signed an agreement whereby both governments agreed to clamp down on each other's insurgents, and batches of ANC personnel were subsequently airlifted to Mozambique and Tanzania. Relations remained tense, but the level of LLA activity dropped off dramatically.

Zimbabwe was not subjected to military intervention, but was dealt to lower level destabilisation measures. In particular, the South African Transport Services made determined efforts to increase that country's dependence upon South Africa by weaning traffic away from Maputo by offering highly competitive rates and facilities to Zimbabwean importers and exporters. South African companies proved increasingly unwilling to ship Zimbabwean goods via Mozambique, and following the sabotage of the Beira-Mutare oil pipeline in early 1983, Pretoria blocked oil imports to Zimbabwe. Meanwhile, South Africa extended shadowy support to various dissident groups with the objective of exacerbating the sharp political tensions which existed between ZANU-PF and the minority Patriotic Front (ZAPU).

In contrast, South Africa's military involvement in Angola and Mozambique was extensive and extremely damaging. Apart from offering direct support to SWAPO and the ANC, both states were ruled by Marxist parties, and constituted a direct ideological challenge to apartheid capitalism.[17] Angola, with its mineral wealth was the country least dependent upon South Africa, and Mozambique, with its ports and harbours, offered trading outlets to SADCC states that were of strategic significance.

Angola was also targeted because of the role it was playing in backing SWAPO. By the late 1970s, South Africa wanted to replace its direct administration in Namibia with a more internationally acceptable internal settlement. Its chosen instrument for this was the Democratic Turnhalle Alliance (DTA), whose task was to forge a coalition of accommodative whites and conservative black leaders which would exclude SWAPO from the political process. An election was held in December 1978; it was boycotted by SWAPO's internal wing and thus resulted in a handsome victory for the DTA. However, the prospects of a viable internal settlement had been dashed by increased SWAPO guerrilla activity from Angola, and considerable efforts were made by the UN

'Contact Group' of five western powers – the United States, Britain, West Germany, France and Canada – to bring South Africa to the negotiating table. These efforts were soon disrupted by the arrival in office of the Reagan administration, which relegated the search for a legitimate Namibian settlement to the periphery of its objectives.

The withering of internal support for the DTA, and the diminution of western pressure upon South Africa to negotiate led to the dismissal of the DTA government and South Africa's reimposition of direct rule in January 1983. Meanwhile, encouraged by the Reagan administration's pursuit of 'linkage', which linked a settlement in Namibia directly to the withdrawal of the Cuban presence from Angola, the SADF appeared to shift to a view that it could win the war against SWAPO by military means. According to the government in Luanda, South African forces violated the Angolan frontier 529 times in the first six months of 1980 alone, and by 1983, the war in southern Angola had escalated into 'high technology, high-casualty, confrontational warfare'. The associated economic and social costs were enormous, with Angola alleging that South African-inflicted destruction had cost them US $10 billion between 1975–82.

In Mozambique, South Africa's chosen instrument of destabilisation was Renamo. From the end of 1981, there was a massive increase in Renamo attacks, and over the next two years US $3,8 billion worth of damage was done to villages, schools, health facilities and government installations. On a number of occasions, Renamo's assaults were directly supported by the SADF, whose special units were responsible for the assassination of a number of ANC activists, such as Ruth First in 1983, while South Africa continued to squeeze the port of Maputo economically. Whereas the initial objective of these destabilisation efforts may have been to overthrow Frelimo, the subsequent realisation was that the installation of a Renamo government would prove immensely costly. As a result the South African objective shifted to that of eroding the Frelimo government's ability to govern.

By the end of 1983, the destabilisation strategy had made considerable gains for South Africa. Swaziland had signed a non-aggression pact; Lesotho had been coerced into expelling the ANC; Zimbabwe had been kept at bay; and Angola and Mozambique had been subjected to immense damage. However, this had been achieved at some considerable cost to Pretoria, for the crudeness of the strategy had begun to embarrass South Africa's western friends. South Africa had gained more freedom of action regionally with the accession to power of the Thatcher government in 1979 and the Reagan administration in 1980. But South African military forays, particularly into Angola, would not have been carried out without the covert backing of Washington. However, by the end of 1983, even the Reagan administration was of the view that destabilisation was creating more dangers for US interests than it was delivering results. Accordingly, from late 1983 the US modified its position by opting for a regional security doctrine, which favoured the recognition of state sovereignty and the cessation of cross-border violence, the control of dissident groups, and the pursuit of regional stability. Meanwhile, the Soviet Union warned Pretoria that it would not tolerate the fall of the MPLA government in Angola, and the apartheid regime began to experience calls from among its own internal supporters for a withdrawal of the SADF. This was after its December 1983 invasion of Angola in 'Operation Askari', which was met by an Angolan military greatly strengthened by the arrival of sophisticated Soviet defence equipment. Not only was the white public jolted but the Angolan war was costing the South African government about US $2 million a day. The result of these diverse pressures was a rapprochement between South Africa and Angola, formalised by the Lusaka Agreement of 16 February 1984 and between South Africa and Mozambique by the Nkomati Agreement, which was signed on 16 March 1984.

(iv) Pax Pretoriana

Davies and O'Meara, writing in 1985, identified the Lusaka and Nkomati Agreements as inaugurating a Pax Pretoriana. In particular, they focussed upon how Pretoria viewed the rapprochement with Mozambique as providing favourable conditions for the relaunching of the constellation initiative, albeit suitably modified. Basically, the Nkomati Agreement committed the Mozambican government to containing the activities of the ANC and South Africa to ending its support for Renamo. A joint security commission was established to monitor the agreement. It was backed by further agreements in the economic sphere, which were intended to illustrate to other countries in the region that co-operation with South Africa paid dividends. These state initiatives were backed by explicit encouragement of the private sector to explore trading and investment opportunities in Mozambique. Meanwhile, the Lusaka Agreement was viewed as indicative of greater willingness by Pretoria to reach a settlement in Namibia. The Nkomati Agreement was seen as offering an opportunity for South Africa to tighten its relations with western powers, and to enable it to emerge as the internationally accepted regional power. Prior to the signing of the Nkomati Agreement, South Africa had infiltrated several hundred Renamo members in Mozambique, and it soon used strong-arm tactics to pressure Lesotho and Botswana to sign formal security agreements. The regional rapprochement envisaged by Pretoria was rapidly being undermined by the conviction of its neighbours that the attainment of real peace was incompatible with the existence of apartheid. Furthermore it was also undermined by the rise of massive popular resistance within South Africa, the South African government's own continued use of destabilisation tactics and, not least, a growing recognition among South Africa's own allies that it was apartheid itself which was at the root of regional instability.

DESTABILISATION AND DÉNOUEMENT

Pretoria had hoped that the Lusaka and Nkomati Agreements would dampen the struggle inside South Africa, lead to cooperative relations with other regional governments, and result in a generalised acceptance throughout the region of South Africa's hegemony and lessen its international isolation. But by mid-1985 it was becoming clear that these objectives were not being realised, leading Pretoria's strategists to conclude that they had less to gain by projecting an image of peaceful intentions towards their neighbours than opting for one of unassailable offensive. Destabilisation and aggression were never abandoned despite the signing of the various non-aggression treaties, and they continued to form the core of South Africa's regional policy.

An early outcome of the policy shift was the displacement of the unco-operative Jonathan regime in Lesotho by a South African-assisted military coup in January 1986. The subsequent military regime of General Justin Lekhanya not only clamped down on a reviving ANC presence, but also happily oversaw the beginning of construction work on the massive Highlands Water Project, whereby mountain waters were to be redirected to the Witwatersand.

With Lesotho co-opted, South Africa conducted the destabilisation strategy on four main fronts. Firstly, albeit at a relatively low level, it extended covert support to Renamo after the latter opened a new front against Zimbabwe, which had despatched troops to Mozambique to defend the Beira railway and oil pipelines, and covertly to assist Renamo's war against Frelimo. Secondly, it continued to offer major support to Unita in Angola. Thirdly, it conducted a series of raids against ANC and other apartheid activists in a number of regional states.

Following the signing of the Lusaka Agreement, Angola had presented a detailed programme for the withdrawal of Cuban troops with the precondition that South Africa must begin implementing UN Resolution 435. The resolution provided for UN supervision of a transitional process to independence in Namibia, and the withdrawal of all its troops from Namibia except 1 500 stipulated in the UN plan. South Africa responded with a proposal that all Cubans leave Angola, with their withdrawal being monitored by a commission, and that South Africans be free to move anywhere in Angola. Subsequently, in April 1985, more than a year after the signing of the Agreement, South Africa made a much publicised withdrawal of troops from Angola, although it stationed two companies to guard hydroelectric plants on the Kunene river. At the same time it announced a new internal government in Namibia, although it left powerful forces on both sides of the Namibian border; and by late 1985 it was heavily involved, with US support, in providing direct military support to Unita.

When the Reagan administration opted to bypass congress restraints by offering covert military assistance to Unita, the SADF became even more heavily involved, eventually launching attacks deep into Angolan territory in May 1986. By this time, South Africa had established a permanent presence in southern Angola, which saw a series of major operations designed to assist Unita take major towns. Then, when in September/October 1987, the Angolans, with support from the Cubans who were now more heavily armed, renewed their offensive against Unita, the SADF weighed in with assistance to the latter which, unusually (and to Savimbi's chagrin), was explicitly admitted and justified by the need to prevent southern Africa from being destabilised and subjected to 'Russian domination'. The announcement of South African involvement was intended, in particular, to appeal to conservative sentiment in the West and at home, but it did reflect a wider concern about the increasing strength of the Angolan and Cuban forces, which were by now armed with sophisticated Soviet equipment. Indeed, the balance of forces was rapidly shifting away from Unita and the SADF, notably in the dimension of air power. Crucially, this was subsequently to be emphasised by the failure of several abortive attempts by the SADF, together with large numbers of the South West African Territory Force and Unita, to inflict a major defeat upon a large Angolan force at Cuito Cuinavale, where they were deployed at distance from their supply lines. Had they been victorious, the SADF and Unita would have been able to extend their presence in southern Angola, and Unita would have held sway over more than a quarter of the country. However, the South African Air Force proved unable to penetrate the Angolan and Cuban defences, while a plan to take the town using ground troops had to be rejected because it was reckoned it would cost the lives of some 300 white conscripts, a price which the regime felt unable to pay. With the war in Angola costing Pretoria some R4 billion a year, the failure to take Cuito Cuanavale constituted a decisive setback which was to produce a new regional conjuncture.

By this time, South Africa had also suffered reverses on the other main fronts of destabilisation. Covert assistance had been extended to Renamo during 1986 and 1987, when groups of several hundreds of the rebels had infiltrated across the South African border with the intention of cutting Mozambique in two. The intention was to relieve Renamo forces in the centre and north of the country which had been subject to major offensives by Frelimo. When this failed, Renamo troops turned their attacks on civilian and road traffic to and from Maputo and on small towns, apparently with the objective of cutting the capital off from the countryside and maximising pressure upon the government by causing a massive displacement of the population. However, despite continued South African assistance, government forces assisted by Tanzanian and Zimbabwean troops began to achieve military victories against Renamo. This happened from late 1987 through 1988, leading to a somewhat improved security situation that ensured that Maputo was never completely cut off from its hinterland. Although the Frelimo government remained unable to inflict a decisive defeat upon the rebels, it was clear by late 1988 that Renamo was in disarray. Three thousand of its members had surrendered and had been granted amnesty, and there was growing evidence that Pretoria's support for the movement's vicious banditry was increasing South Africa's international isolation and causing acute concern in the West. But overall, the situation remained a stalemate, rendering the Mozambique government and its allies increasingly desperate for a settlement – this indicated *inter alia* by the withdrawal in November 1988 of Tanzanian troops, who had been assisting Frelimo since the previous year.[19]

Meanwhile, the third leg of the destabilisation strategy had begun to run into trouble. South Africa had continued to launch raids and assassination attempts upon members of the ANC located in neighbouring countries. Many of these attacks involved the death or injury not of South African exiles but of nationals of the countries concerned. For instance, during the period February 1984 to February 1985, Botswana was subject to 20 direct SADF attacks, 37 lesser incidents involving incursions or cross-border shootings and 23 known air space violations. Despite SADF claims that every effort was made to target ANC 'terrorists', only 10 of the 31 people killed in these attacks were South Africans, and the majority were refugees.[20] These attacks damaged South Africa's image, notably when the SADF raided Gaborone in 1986 during the visit to South Africa by the Commonwealth Eminent Persons Group, a last-ditch effort by that body to see if apartheid could be brought to an end by mediation. During 1988 the campaign extended to Europe, with the assassination of Dulcie September, the ANC representative in Paris, and the attempts upon her counterpart in Brussels.

The late 1980s set the scene set for the final dénouement – and led to the adoption by Pretoria of more flexible foreign policies, allowing a more dove-like element (centred around Foreign Minister Pik Botha) to win over the more hawkish establishment led by Defence Minister General Magnus Malan. Three factors were of particular importance. First, the impact of sanctions and international isolation on the Republic's economy were making it necessary to reforge Pretoria's image; second, the war in Angola, culminating in the battle at Cuito Cuanavale, was becoming increasingly expensive (both financially and in white lives); and third, Soviet leader Mikhail Gorbachev's new policies with their emphasis on reducing the USSR's role in regional conflicts contributed to creating a new international climate, and reduced Pretoria's obsessions about a 'total onslaught' by communism.[21] In turn, the shift to a less adversarial relationship between the Soviet Union and the United States with regard to regional conflicts reduced Pretoria's importance to Washington, while simultaneously presenting the South African government with a unique opportunity to overcome its diplomatic isolation and gain a new global legitimacy by moving towards more constructive relations with neighbouring states – and, not least, the ANC.

The increasing pressure of sanctions was one factor encouraging South Africa to look at expanding trade and investment links with the rest of Africa. Indeed, trade with African countries was said to have increased by 40 per cent in 1986 and by 37 per cent in 1987, and continued to rise thereafter.[22] This was illustrated by the forging of considerably closer economic ties with Mozambique, whose relationship with South Africa now became 'perplexingly contradictory': while elements within the South African security apparatus (with or without the knowledge of the government) continued to give direct assistance to Renamo, formal relations between the two governments strengthened. The (suspended) Joint Security Commission established under the Nkomati Accord was reactivated in September 1988 at a meeting between PW Botha and President Chissano at Songo, and the revitalisation of a Joint Economic Commission in February 1989 matched a series of initiatives which *inter alia* saw the Anglo-American Corporation showing interest to develop natural gas fields off the Mozambican coast, South Africa agreeing to rebuild the 500 pylons on the Cabora Bassa electricity line destroyed by Renamo, and agreements to rehabilitate Maputo port, and the railway line and road between Maputo and the South African border, and the lifting of a partial ban on the recruitment of Mozambican workers to the South African mines. Subsequently, the succession of FW de Klerk to the South African presidency, and the domestic reforms which he soon initiated, encouraged the Mozambican government to believe that the era of destabilisation was soon to be over. Furthermore Nelson Mandela's pledge after his release from jail in early 1990 that a post-apartheid government would consider paying reparations to the region seemed to inaugurate a new era of co-operation. Yet this was not to be, and South Africa's relations with Mozambique continued to be flawed by a fundamental ambiguity until both countries eventually progressed to their first democratic elections in 1994.

More certain progress was made with regard to Angola and Namibia. By 1988, Gorbachev's attempts to grapple with the mounting problems of the Soviet economy had forced the Soviet Union to reassess its commitments in Africa, and to press the ANC into accepting a negotiated settlement. In turn, South Africa began to realise that a SWAPO government in Namibia would no longer pose a threat so long as the Cubans were persuaded to leave the region. Meanwhile, although 'Marxist', neither Mozambique, thoroughly weakened by war, nor Zimbabwe had proved able to pose an effective challenge to South Africa. At the same time, however, South Africa was rapidly losing its friends. With the decline of the Soviet threat globally, the US viewed South

Africa less as an ally than as a cause of regional instability. This international hostility had led to the increasingly tight application of economic sanctions. Realising that the concession of Namibia could now be made at relatively little cost, South Africa entered into a series of talks with the US, Angola and Cuba. These talks resulted in an agreement in August 1988, which led to a South African withdrawal from Angola on the last day of that month. A final agreement was eventually signed on 22 December, and April 1989 was set as the date for the implementation of UN Resolution 435 and the transition of Namibia to independence. A separate bilateral agreement signed by Cuba and Angola stipulated the procedure for the phased withdrawal of Cuban forces from Angola, which began in January 1989 and which was to be completed by July 1991.[23] The scene was thereby set for SWAPO's eventual triumph in a UN supervised election in December 1989, followed by the withdrawal of South African forces from Namibia, and SWAPO's assumption of power at Namibia's independence on 21 March 1990.

With the changes wrought by Mikhail Gorbachev, both domestically and internationally, Pretoria's military strategy of engaging in total war against 'communism's total onslaught' had lost justification. Importantly too, the change in the international climate brought about the end of the Soviet Union's status as a superpower, and made it possible for the Afrikaner establishment to accept the demise of apartheid and the need to face up to the prospect of majority rule. This led to the final removal from office of the hardline PW Botha in favour of FW de Klerk in August 1989, and the latter's unbanning of the liberation movements in his historic speech of 2 February 1990. Many difficulties were to precede the progression to democracy in April 1994, but from that moment, South Africa's days as a militaristic rogue elephant in Africa were over.

CONCLUSION

South Africa's accession to democracy in 1994 provided the opportunity for the country to play a very different and obviously more constructive role in Africa than during the dark days of apartheid. Although the National Party participated in the newly elected Government of National Unity, it was the ANC's agenda which now governed its foreign policy, with the search for peace and human rights being adopted as its principal guidelines. Although the 'new South Africa' was accorded an extremely warm welcome into the international community of nations, its opportunities in Africa were necessarily shaped by the legacy of what had happened before. For all its good intentions, the new government could not – and is not – fully able to shake off its inheritance.[24]

Although South Africa is now a proud member of the reshaped Southern African Development Community (SADC), which has replaced SADCC, the rapid invasion of the African hinterland by South African corporate capital is opening it to charges that it is becoming an economic hegemon. And equally, although South Africa has been careful to locate its regional political initiatives in terms of SADC policies, false moves – such as the bungling of its military intervention to shore up the elected government in Lesotho in 1998 – have opened it up to the charge from some quarters that it is all too disposed to throw its weight around. However, whatever legitimacy critiques of current foreign policy may possess, they pale into insignificance when the sheer evil and destruction that was wrought by the previous regime during the final, dying days of apartheid are remembered. The challenge to South Africa is to repair the damage done in the past to its neighbouring states by forging constructive relations and helping to promote continental development and security.

---

1 This paper is largely a reworking of Southall (1984), and is also heavily dependent upon Davies and O'Meara (1985).
2 Nolutshungu, S (1975) *South Africa in Africa: A study of Ideology and foreign policy.* Manchester: Manchester University Press.
3 Jaster, R (1985) 'South Africa's narrowing Security Options' in Jaster, R (ed) *Southern Africa: Regional Security Problems and Prospects.* Aldershot: Gower. 37– 87.
4 Ibid. p 29.
5 Southall, R (1984).
6 O'Meara, D (1983) *Volks Kapitalisme: Class, Capital and Ideology in the Development of Afrikaner Nationalism 1934–1948.* Johannesburg: Ravan Press.
7 Spence, J.E (1965) *Republic Under Pressure: a Study of South African Foreign Policy.* London: Oxford University Press.
8 Walker, E.A (1962) *A History of Southern Africa.* London: Longman.
9 Tomlinson, (1955).
10 Nolutshungu, S (1975) *South Africa in Africa: A study of Ideology and foreign policy.* Manchester: Manchester University Press.
11 Molteno, R (1971) 'South Africa's Forward Policy in Africa: milestones on the Great North Road', *The Round Table,* 243, 1971: pp 329–345.
12 Nolutshungu, S (1975) *South Africa in Africa: A study of ideology and foreign policy.* Manchester: Manchester University Press.
13 Legum, C (1975) *The Secret Diplomacy of Detente, p* 12.
14 Davies and O'Meara 1985: p 185.
15 ibid.
16 Southall and Woods (1998) pp 120–122.
17 op. cit.
18 Barber J and Barratt J (1990) *South Africa's Foreign Policy: the search for status and security 1945–1988.* Cambridge; Cambridge University Press: pp 341–342.
19 Legum C (1992) 'The Southern African Crisis: The Tide Begins to Turn', in Legum C and Doro, M (Eds) *Africa Contemporary Record* Vol. 21, *1988–89.* p. A19.

20 Johnson, P and Martin, D *Apartheid Terrorism: The Destabilization Report.* London, Bloomington and Indianapolis: The Commonwealth Secretariat.
21 Legum and Doro (Eds) *Africa Contemporary Record 1988–89:B719.*
22 ibid:B720.
23 ibid:B556–557; Grundy K.(1991) *South Africa: Domestic Crisis and Global Challenge.* Boulder, Colorado; Westview Press, pp 115–116.
24 Bischoff, P-H and Southall, R (1999) ?The Early Foreign Policy of the Democratic South Africa, in Wright, S (Ed), *African Foreign Policies.* Boulder, Colorado: Westview Press, pp. 154–181.

PART TWO:
THE AFRICA POLICIES OF FRANCE AND SOUTH AFRICA

PART TWO

Chapter Three:

THE REFORM OF FRENCH POLICY IN AFRICA: MODERNISING AND OPENING UP[1]

Roland Dubertrand

The ongoing reform of French policy in Africa takes place at a time when Paris and Pretoria are committing themselves to closer political co-operation since the first conference of this kind in 1993. With different contexts and different situations, both countries are now faced with the necessity of implementing changes in their approach to Africa, in order to take into account the developments we have seen on the continent since the beginning of the decade.

As far as France is concerned, African policy has to be seen as a part of our global foreign policy. This may sound obvious but it is often forgotten. After the independence of the African states, General de Gaulle saw in the system of co-operation which was then put into place an opportunity not only to express our faithfulness to these countries and to be present on the continent, but also an opportunity to enhance the world status of our country, particularly as an advocate of the new North-South relations. So today there is no doubt that our decisive commitment to Europe implies that France should integrate her special relationship with Africa into the wider European context, and that the characteristics of future ties between Europe and Africa remain to be precisely defined.

Furthermore, it seems that France has no vital strategic interests in sub-Saharan Africa (the same does not apply to North Africa). Indeed, the developments in the sub-Saharan region can hardly endanger France's existence and independence. But, at the same time, black Africa does play a substantial role in our internal policy, in accordance with our past and present commitments. The immigrant communities from sub-Saharan Africa do not weigh as much as those from Algeria, Morocco and Tunisia, but the political class and the opinion leaders are bound by a tight network of personal relationships and reciprocal influences. Beyond the image of a 'big family', based on a romantic perception of lasting friendships, it is important to understand that the idea of a 'withdrawal' of France from Africa cannot stand up against proper political analysis, especially if one takes into account the realities of politics and diplomacy. Quite the opposite in fact is true: the 1990s led to an 'adaptation' of our policy, long overdue. I would like to explain why and how, before venturing into some considerations which will also deal with South Africa.

THE POST-COLONIAL SYSTEM AND THE REFORM: THE TRANSITION YEARS

France did not enforce her nature in 1960 when 15 African states decided to leave the French community. As Jean-François Bayart explains, the aim after independence was to consolidate the young state apparatuses, through widespread co-operation in the technical and development fields, based on the same model of 'state control and protectionism' which had held sway since 1930. Infrastructure, education, public administration were on the agenda. Priority was given to the stability of the states and leaders in power and this was achieved, for instance, through defence and military co-operation agreements. At the time each side found its own benefit in this system, except perhaps for the paternalistic relationship which such a system tends to encourage. The system was not threatened by the fall of the Berlin Wall; it was the developments in Africa themselves which forced the changes: the democratic ideals appearing among the urban classes at the end of the 1980s; the deep economic crisis of this decade and its impact on state intervention which had bred bad administration and corruption; and a stronger surge of nationalism since the 1970s.

The changes took place in two phases: as early as 1990, President Mitterand adopted the principle of 'aid against democracy', at the La Baule summit; four years later, with the so-called 'Abidjan doctrine' on structural adjustment, France required good economic governance as a condition for aid, and the CFA franc was devaluated. Again in 1994, the Rwandan genocide and the fall of Mobutu in 1997, two very different incidents in this evolution, but they took place in a region, the Great Lakes, where French interests were not the highest – in fact a caricature was made of France's positions regarding these crises. However the consequences in terms of credibility encouraged us to do some introspection.

Paris drew the conclusion that the time for external intervention was over and that western powers had to take other responsibilities in an increasingly autonomous Africa. It remains a fact, however, that the French presence contributed to a greater degree of peace and stability in the relevant regions than anywhere else on the continent.

In this context, the modernisation and adaptation of French policy in Africa was decided upon and implemented by the French authorities towards the end of 1997 and the beginning of this year. I will briefly explain the four principles on which the reform is based:

1. The unilateral intervention in internal affairs has been discarded, but the defence agreements have been retained against external aggression. The accent has been placed on peace-keeping operations, as evidenced by the RECAMP programme (Enhancement of African Peacekeeping Capacities) and the tripartite initiative launched by France, Great Britain and the United States.
2. The partnership with French-speaking countries has been maintained and modernised but, at the same time, France is open to co-operation with the whole of Africa, particularly South Africa and Angola.
3. The system of co-operation and aid for development has been maintained and restructured, but French attention is concentrated on the poorest countries (identified as the 'priority solidarity zone'). This includes special consideration for human rights issues and democracy. Furthermore, the Ministry of Co-operation is being integrated into the Ministry of Foreign Affairs, in order to obtain an optimal coherence of French external policy.
4. The European dimension of French policy has been taken more into account; the priority here has been the renewal of

the Lomé convention and the linking of the CFA franc to the Euro; another priority has been to co-ordinate French actions with multilateral institutions and the other donors, for instance, Japan to take an example outside Europe.

The challenge is a major one, especially if one considers that 50 per cent of French public aid is dedicated to sub-Saharan Africa, that is R18 billion this year. France is Africa's first partner, not only in terms of aid, but also in terms of trade and military co-operation.

The reform is now being implemented. The next question is what impact will it have on the relations between France and Africa?

NEW CHALLENGES FOR A NEW TYPE OF PRESENCE ON THE CONTINENT

Once again, we must rectify the simplistic perceptions spread by some English-speaking media that French presence in Africa declined between 1994 and 1997, and that this decline is only a prelude to a total disengagement. For my part, I cannot see any sign of retreat, but rather an adjustment to a new era and an extension to the whole of Africa. The complexity of recent military conflicts that have taken place on the continent has shown that Africa is not the stage of a Manichean drama, where the 'goods' – new leaders, advocates of democracy and market economy – annihilate the 'bads' – corrupted dictators – by throwing them into the pits of history. There are no geo-strategic and linguistic blocs either, but various states freed from the constraints of the Cold War and the burden of apartheid. Some of these states are achieving the successful consolidation of their structures and involvement on the international scene, others not. The challenge for external partners is how to deal with all of them.

France wishes to establish or develop a solid partnership with emerging countries, without forgetting the very poor countries that are still fighting against the grip of underdevelopment. The economic growth rate of these past few years has been quite remarkable for many states. We also know that the Great Lakes crisis, raging since 1994, can have tremendous repercussions and only persistent effort will be able to solve the crisis. The countries in the region bear the first responsibility for trying to solve it. France has welcomed the initiatives by South Africa – since the

Pretoria summit – as well as those of other neutral states and regional organisations.

If a proper regional compromise and a wide political dialogue within the DRC are to be attained, we believe the international community should also support this effort, give guarantees, participate in peacekeeping and in economic reconstruction. This is why Paris proposed that an international conference could be organised at an opportune time, if this proposition is agreeable to the Africans themselves.

I have already mentioned the fact that France's major areas of interest, including the spheres of economy and energy, are not the Great Lakes, but rather West Africa, the Gulf of Guinea and increasingly the SADC region. However, our completely neutral stance in the current central African crisis does not mean a lack of interest, but the opposite in fact. Paris wishes to be able to deal with a stable and peaceful Congo, with territorial unity and an efficient and democratic state apparatus.

It is also essential to correct once and for all the perception that a so-called rivalry between France and the United States exists in Africa. This perception feeds on a *presumed* antagonism between French and English-speaking Africa. Companies from the two countries, and from other countries too, compete on the ground; there is nothing more normal in today's world market. However, it is much more speculative and in fact incorrect to draw the conclusion that an implacable and systematic political rivalry takes place. France is attached to her independence of action, although within the context of an ever-growing European integration, and attached to the *'francophonie'*. We will continue to plead, in the international arena, for a model of development which takes into account the national characteristics of a country and the responsibilities of its state, facing the consequences of neo-liberalism. In Africa as anywhere else, co-operation with the United States is possible on many issues. I would like to cite as an example the project around the Enhancement of Peacekeeping Capacities. In addition, real differences, like we have had on the Sudan or the former Zaire, do not end up as hostilities when Paris and Washington can discuss them openly. What we do want to change are the prejudices which prevail and which stop people from considering the positive aspects of the French presence in Africa. France has brought more than her share to Africa, as far as solidarity, aid for development, peace support and stability are concerned. And we will continue to do so. Today, we want to work with the whole continent, without forgetting our traditional allies, and with any external partner who refuses, like us, to see Africa marginalised.

FRANCE AND SOUTH AFRICA

All that I have just said applies to the relations between our two countries. One must simply keep in mind that South Africa is an African power, and France is an external partner, albeit a close one.

All signs are there that South Africa is playing and will play a crucial role in the future of the continent, both in economic and political terms; the country will assess its position in the SADC region and in the context of a wider vision of the continent. The best method of co-operation is probably to take each situation individually and study where the two countries could assist in terms of development or conflict resolution. For instance, in the Comoros or the Great Lakes conflict which certainly calls for consultation.

In a word, conditions are ripe today, thanks to the concept of the African renaissance and to the desire of France to enter a new era of relationships with the continent, to become more aware of our simultaneous autonomy and interdependence.

---

1   This chapter was written in November 1998 and reflects the situation at that time.

Chapter Four:

SOUTH AFRICA'S AFRICA POLICY[1]

Aziz Pahad

Five years since the birth of our democracy the reality that we are not a European outpost on the African continent, but an African country whose destiny is inextricably linked to that of our continent is fast gaining momentum. Despite the recent resurgence in 'Afro-pessimism' one cannot indulge in the luxury of scepticism and despondency, but ought constructively and critically to examine the challenges facing Africa. I have been asked to deal with South Africa's policy towards Africa, specifically, with its role in the conflictual situations in the Democratic Republic of the Congo and Angola, as well as in Lesotho; South Africa and the Southern African Development Community; and, finally to contextualise South African foreign policy in terms of the African renaissance.

SOUTH AFRICAN FOREIGN POLICY AND THE AFRICAN RENAISSANCE

Historically and especially in the post-colonial period African leaders spoke of Africa's contributions to the very evolution of human life and also of ancient times when Africa was the leading centre of learning, technology and culture. They also called for an African reawakening. The vision was there, the time was not right.

Today, as we prepare to enter the new millennium, there is a renewed spirit of confidence and self-assertiveness on our continent. Africans are again asking questions, *inter alia*, why, despite our enormous potential, are the greatest number of least developing countries found in Africa (33 out of 48), why did sub-Saharan Africa's slice of the world trade fall from three per cent in the mid-1950s and to one per cent in 1995; why have African exports fallen by 50 per cent from 1985 to 1995; why do the living standards of the vast majority of people continue to decline, and infant mortality remain shockingly high; why are we burdened with massive external debts; why do we continue to suffer from unstable political systems, characterised by one-party systems, dictators, and military rule which has resulted in conflicts, civil wars, genocide and the emergence of millions of refugees.

President Thabo Mbeki noted that, 'There exists within our continent a generation which has been victim to all things which created the negative past: this generation remains African and carries with it a historic pride which compels it to seek a place for Africans equal to all other peoples of our common universe.' There is no need to spend endless hours intellectualising about the meaning of an 'African renaissance' or whether it is a new or an old concept. Simply put it is a challenge to ensure that

- we move from one-party states to multi-party democracies;
- we establish systems of good governance, and respect for human rights and democracy;
- we create people-centred societies that will ensure that the people are empowered to determine their own destiny. This demands that we give increasing attention to the building of institutions of government and society. It also demands that we give concrete expression to the empowerment of women;
- we move away from state-controlled economies and achieve sustainable development. The basic objective of this must be the elimination of poverty and reduction of the gap between the rich and the poor (between countries and within countries). To achieve this it will be necessary to deal with neo-colonial relations, distorted macro-economic policies, commodity-based economies, closed and over-protected economies, small markets, heavy debt burdens, inadequate infrastructure and a low skills base;
- we end conflicts;
- and, finally, we reject coups.

We seek to achieve all this in a new world order that has changed dramatically in the last few years. Not only do we have to deal with the legacies of the past, but now we are confronted with the phenomenon of globalisation, liberalisation, deregulation and the information super-highway. Today five companies control more than 50 per cent of the global market in fields such as the automotive industry, aerospace, electricity and electronics. Five corporations control more than 40 per cent of the global market in computers and the media. Three hundred and fifty of the world's largest corporations now account for 40 per cent of the global trade. Total global income has increased sixfold since 1960. But more than half the world's population has to support themselves on less than two dollars a day.

Increasingly the sovereignty of national states is being eroded and our capacity to take major economic, political and social decisions is impacted upon. It is therefore crucial that we seek to achieve Africa's renewal on a solid foundation based on strong subregional groupings.

SOUTH AFRICA AND REGIONAL DEVELOPMENT IN SOUTHERN AFRICA

On 29 August 1994, South Africa joined the Southern African Development Community (SADC), firmly committing itself to the development and integration of the region. A few days later at a EU/SADC conference in Berlin, then Foreign Minister Alfred Nzo summed up South Africa's vision for the SADC as 'Peace, Prosperity, and Partnership' and as the newly elected chairman of SADC, my vision remains essentially the same for South Africa today. It would be appropriate, however, to look frankly at some of the problems confronting our vision and at how South Africa plans to address them.

In determining a vision for SADC, from a South African perspective, it is necessary first to understand the South African approach as set out in the policy document describing the relation between South Africa and the countries of the southern African region. As a member of SADC, South Africa is committed to contribute to the best of its ability to the improvement of life for all of SADC and its people. We are committed to intra-regional relations based on peace and orientated towards sustainable development and economic growth. The emphasis is therefore on the effective distribution and management of existing resources.

To this end our vision for the southern African region is one of the highest possible degree of economic co-operation, mutual assistance where necessary and joint planning of regional development initiatives, leading to integration consistent with socio-economic, environmental and political realities. South Africa will contribute through mutual benefit and interdependence to regional co-operation and integration and not through 'power politics'. South Africa and its people are partners to the reconstruction and development of SADC, as the people and countries in SADC were partners in the liberation of South Africa. We will work towards the maximisation of each country's potential in the region, taking into account the principles and guidelines of the Organisation of African Unity – equality, mutual benefit and peaceful coexistence.

As a newcomer to the formal regional grouping, we were greatly honoured and encouraged when we were elected to chair the organisation for the next three years. We will work to maintain and increase the momentum towards the establishment of an economic community built up through the period in which SADC was chaired by Botswana. As chair we have committed ourselves to the furtherance of the objectives of SADC through closer regional co-operation and integration. We specifically commit ourselves to contribute in a collective way to implement the objects set out by SADC and to build the community and strengthen it both economically and politically. We believe that the point has now been reached at which a higher degree of integration is a necessary precondition for further SADC development and that in the strengthening of democratic mechanisms, the partnership between governments and the non-governmental sectors is an increasing priority.

We wish to maintain the proud character and tradition which form the building blocks of SADC, this unique African approach to regional co-operation and integration, an approach which stresses decentralised participation by member countries, as well as equity, mutual benefit and balance. We believe that SADC has made an important contribution to forging a regional identity and sense of common destiny among the countries and people of southern Africa and intend to build on these solid foundations.

In the implementation of the objectives of the SADC treaty, it is our intention to further enhance regional decision taking by consensus. We also wish to involve by way of direct community involvement, inclusivity and transparency, the people of the region in the process of regional integration. We feel that it is imperative that the regional order be developed by the people of the region. All stakeholders (non-governmental organisations, civic organisations, governments, parastatals, development agencies, private sector, unions, etc) should together shape the future of southern Africa. Furthermore, development of the region is not about the allocation of South African and foreign resources to the countries of the region, but rather it is about the active involvement and empowerment of the southern African people in determining how their resources and energies are utilised to their own maximum benefit.

In the carrying out of our functions as chair of SADC, we are extremely fortunate in being able to draw on the experience of Mozambique, or vice-chair. In collaboration with Mozambique and the SADC Executive Secretary, we intend setting up a joint management mechanism to assist in the process of determining priorities and setting direction for the further development of our region. We will give specific priority to areas and activities where the harmonisation of activities and the development of sector and/or issue specific protocols and agreements will promote cross-border activity and economic integration and, with that, a more balanced regional development pattern. To this end we are seriously committed to the implementation of the protocols signed in 1995 and 1996, namely the shared watercourses, trade, energy, transport and communications, and illicit drug trafficking agreements, as well as the Southern African Power Pool Agreement.

SADC has now embraced a wider agenda for integration that incorporates both project development and market integration. We need to adapt to the demands of the rapidly changing world economy and to develop the skills needed to compete internationally. We should be very clear that our aim is that the domestic economic policies of all southern African states should be in harmony, facilitating the design of a regional trade regime and greater sector co-operation in the economic field.

Being serious about regional co-operation and integration means that it is crucial that we must go beyond our policy of co-ordinating national initiatives. Regional co-operation must become a daily experience in the management of our national affairs. In our opinion, this requires a system of management that ensures and accommodates an integrated approach where these objectives are maintained on a continuous basis. Such an approach will avoid potential imbalances in resource allocation to individual sectors and will also make provision for a re-prioritisation of resource allocations. South Africa is concerned about the need for enhancing the capacity within the SADC structures to co-ordinate all developmental activities to allow for synergy and coherence. The organisation has so far not been able to mobilise to the fullest extent possible the region's own resources for development. Yet this is one of the central objectives, as well as strategies, for effective and self-sustaining regional development. In addition, SADC's dependence on donor countries and its neglect of local and regional capital markets contradicts the two principal aims of SADC – the mobilisation of members' own resources and the lessening of economic dependence upon others. In order to correct this, there is a need for greater political commitment as well as effective institutions and mechanisms to mobilise own resources.

We have noted with appreciation the Review and Rationalisation of the SADC Programme of Action, especially the enhancement of the capacity for overall regional planning, programme management, assessment and co-ordination within the community, but are aware of a lack of determination and capacity to translate the logic of regional co-ordination and planning into the national decision-making process of member states.

The different sector co-ordination units, although to a large degree integrated into the national administration of the SADC member states responsible for those sectors, are in almost every instance removed from the national decision-making process. In many instances, the sector co-ordinating units and corresponding sector contact points are scarcely consulted when preparations are afoot to make national decisions concerning projects in the sector concerned. This dichotomy between 'thinking national' and 'thinking regional' is apparent when one considers that although all states have signed the Convention on De-certification, only six have ratified it; only Botswana, Lesotho, Mauritius and South Africa have ratified the Protocol on Shared Water Course Systems and only Mauritius has ratified the Trade Protocol.

We feel it is important that all member countries should participate actively in the process of identifying regional priorities, and would like to propose that, as a first step in this direction, we should commission a comprehensive regional assessment on, *inter alia*, the regional demography; human, natural and mineral resources; infrastructure and services. Unfortunately there is a lack of clear national perspective outlining individual member states; strategic interests in regional integration and co-operation. As a result, member states have not been successful in articulating and demonstrating the benefits of regional co-operation to their citizens. The problem will be difficult to address completely, as neither the organisation nor its member states has the institutional capacity or the financial resources to sustain the process of consultation and mobilisation of stakeholders at the national level.

The regional resources assessment will, nevertheless, assist SADC in the establishment of a macro-framework, whereby the Community could identify specific short, medium and long-term priorities towards regional co-operation and integration. We feel that there should be alignment at sectoral level and within the secretariat with the above priorities. A grave cause for concern, formally noted at the Council of Minister's meeting in Windhoek last month, is that SADC structures at national level, in particular national contact points, sectoral contact points and national media co-ordinators are too week to effectively engage relevant national stakeholders in the organisation's activities and programmes and national structures will have to be revamped as a matter of priority. We obviously need to re-focus our attention on the all important aspect of human resource development in the southern African region. As stated in the SADC treaty, the most binding constraint to the development of the region is inadequate professionally and technically qualified and experienced personnel to plan and manage the development process efficiently and effectively. We define human resource development as the lifelong process of developing an individual's potential to the fullest, through education and training, improved health, the ability to earn a decent living, the exercise of economic and political choices, and guaranteed basic human rights, to afford him/her full involvement in the development process.

Turning to the issue of regional security, it should be emphasised that, for economic growth and development to thrive, a prerequisite is peace and stability in southern Africa. To achieve lasting peace and security, we should actively promote our foreign policy principles in southern Africa and should encourage our brother countries to promote human rights and democracy. Without democracy, freedom and respect for human rights – the pillars of our approach to international relations – durable peace and stability cannot be realised. In this regard we should strengthen the security and defence forums within the southern African region. Common security arrangements could facilitate the sharing of information, intelligence and resources, the early warning of potential crises, joint problem solving, implementing confidence and security-building measures, as well as preventative measures and mechanisms in support of peace and stability.

The responsibility for this falls under the Organ for Politics, Defence and Security by way of the inclusion of the already functioning Inter State Security and Defence Committee. Although no final picture has yet emerged as to how the political function of the

Organ will operate, South Africa expects that this body will be responsible for political dialogue with other regional organisations, concentrating on issues of common concern, while the current SADC will be responsible for socio-economic development. This will mean that a number of the established responsibilities and relationships, for example the Berlin Initiative with the EU, the SADC/Nordic and the SADC/ASEAN dialogues, will fall under the ambit of the Organ. SADC and the EU agreed in October 1996 to combat and end the indiscriminate use and spread throughout the world of anti-personnel landmines as well as to contribute to solving the problems already caused by these weapons. SADC, as a region cursed with this scourge, has taken the initiative in calling for a worldwide mobilisation of support for de-mining in the affected countries. You will be aware that South Africa announced it would prohibit the use, development, production and stockpiling of anti-personnel land-mines with immediate effect. This announcement placed South Africa among the leaders in the prohibition of these weapons, an example of how regional initiative should interact with national legislation to the benefit of all.

Apart from the identified priority areas on which SADC should concentrate on the short term (human resource development, the further development of the SADC Organ, the rationalisation of the SADC Programme of Action and community building), gender equality should also receive attention in all the activities of SADC. To this end it is important to mention that the Council of Ministers approved the establishment of a gender unit in the SADC Secretariat during the Consultative Conference on Nambia on 7 February 1997.

South Africa believes that the region can achieve its full potential only through close co-operation in the exploitation of natural resources in a co-ordinated fashion, the pooling of technical expertise, the harmonisation of trade practice and the promotion of the economies of scale. To this end it chose to utilise the instrument already at hand, the Southern African Development Community, and we believe that despite deficiencies, SADC's organisation and structures provide valuable opportunities for enhancing the growth and prosperity of all the countries of the region.

The most important challenge confronting SADC today is to generate a synergy between the economies of the region; we must renegotiate the SACU agreement; through a combination of sectoral co-operation, policy co-ordination and trade integration, South Africa's regional policy must aim to achieve a dynamic regional economy capable of effectively competing in the global economy. Currently negotiations are taking place to (i) achieve

agreement for our asymmetrical free trade area; (ii) link regional trade development and industrial restructuring; (iii) promote co-ordinated infrastructure and resource-based industrial development; (iv) encourage South African investments in the region through a further relation of foreign exchange controls; (v) promote regional trade facilitation, and strengthen customs control and administration. We must also seek a common SADC approach to issues such as international crime and terrorism, drug syndicates, the proliferation of small arms, democratisation of the system of international governance, Aids and environmental degradation. Thus South Africa's vision for SADC could be summarised as:
- The development of a sustainable and politically secure,
- economic community in terms of the SADC Treaty and
- within the framework of the Abuja Treaty.

SOUTH AFRICA AND CONFLICT RESOLUTION IN AFRICA

One of the most important objectives of our foreign policy in Africa, and one that builds upon the structures and institutions of regionalism, must be that of conflict resolution. The Secretary General of the United Nations (UN), Kofi Annan, in a major report to the UN on conflicts in Africa stated that:

> Conflict in Africa poses a major challenge to UN efforts designed to ensure global peace, prosperity and human rights. The UN is being required more and more often to respond to intrastate stability and conflict. In those conflicts the main aim increasingly is the destruction not just of armies but of civilians and entire ethnic groups. Preventing such wars is no longer a matter of defending states or protecting allies. It is a matter of defending humanity itself.

For South Africa, the persistence of conflict within the SADC ambit poses the most immediate and pervasive challenge to its vision of an African renewal.

Today in the Democratic Republic of Congo (DRC), South Africa is facing one of the greatest dangers since the post-colonial period. The danger of an African war is frighteningly real. Since the rebellion against the Kabila government broke out in August 1998, we are confronted with the stark reality that troops from Zimbabwe, Angola, Namibia, Chad and Sudan are fighting on the side of rebels. Furthermore, other countries are being lobbied to intervene militarily as are 'non-statutory forces' (described by some as the 'Garbage of Africa') such as the Interahamwe, ex-Rwandan and Burundi armed forces, ex-Mobutu forces, armed formations of Congo Brazzaville and Unita. The accusations and counter-accusations of ethnic cleansing, coupled with the continuing threat to the security of Uganda and Rwanda, act to stoke further the fires of conflict.

The origins of the problem lie with the Mobutu regime, the role of its international sponsors and its inability to meet the challenge of a changing international and continental environment. With the onset of a rebellion against the dying leader, a loose alliance of anti-Mobutu forces supported by the Rwandese military swept the dictator out of power and took control of the country. From South Africa's perspective, the collapse of the anti-Mobutu alliance and the current conflagration are an illustration of the debilitating legacy of Mobutu and, concurrently, the dangers of taking power by the barrel of the gun. The geographic division of the country along Kabila and anti-Kabila lines, the scramble for resources and the humanitarian crisis which accompanies the conflict represents a tragedy equalling that of the original Congo crisis which brought Mobutu to power in the early 1960s.

South Africa's perspective on the crisis in the DRC is one that has been consistently in support of a negotiated settlement from the outset. From the talks at Victoria Falls to the Pretoria summit of August 1998, South African diplomacy has sought to encourage all parties to cease hostilities and begin discussions towards resolving the conflict. Stated briefly, its strategic objectives are

- to win acceptance of the principle that sovereignty and territorial integrity of countries must be respected;
- to secure recognition of Laurent Kabila as the sole legitimate government of the DRC;
- to develop a shared understanding of the nature of the problem in its external and in its internal manifestations;
- to convey a sense of urgency on participants of the necessity of finding a negotiated solution to the crisis.

South Africa has called for an immediate cessation of hostilities, troop standstill, and a negotiated ceasefire agreement. This would be followed by the withdrawal of foreign troops and their replacement by an international peacekeeping force under the auspices of the Organisation of African Unity (OAU) and UN Security Council. Finally, this must be complemented by the opening of an all-inclusive political dialogue within the DRC. These perspectives endorsed at various other summits, including a meeting in Addis Ababa in September 1998 where an agreement on the modalities for effecting an immediate ceasefire and the mechanisms for monitoring compliance with the ceasefire provisions was reached. The primary stumbling block remains, however, the absence of key figures in the anti-Kabila alliance, that is Rwanda, Uganda, and the rebels themselves.

In spite of these difficulties, South Africa remains committed to a negotiated solution to the conflict in the DRC. Indeed, the strategic importance of the DRC to SADC and the continent as a whole render any prolongation of the conflict potentially disastrous. The impact of the crisis has already been felt on Angola, where the commitment of Luanda's military forces and the concurrent involvement of Unita added yet another dimension to that country's grievous war. The economic and social consequences of conducting armed operations by the various regional participants, many of whom are expending resources which are needed elsewhere, are being felt by their domestic constituents. And, finally, the human tragedy of the onset of a new cycle of refugees must be addressed if the conditions for peace and prosperity are to prevail.

Turning to another issue of grave concern to South Africa and the region, and one in which South Africa and its SADC partners took decisive action, that of the Lesotho constitutional crisis. The coup conducted on 16 September 1998 was the sixth in Lesotho since 1970. Observers will recall that when a coup took place in 1994, SADC took unequivocal action and strongly condemned it. Diplomatic initiatives coupled with the real threat of SADC military intervention led to the end of the mutiny and the restoration of democracy. Sadly a mere four years later junior officers carried out another coup. All efforts to end the mutiny through negotiations failed. It became obvious that without the normalisation of the security situation, the impasse in the political negotiations could not be broken, and the political, economic, social and security situation continued to deteriorate.

In these circumstances SADC had no alternative but to intervene militarily. The South African National Defence Force (SANDF) has made an unprecedented, transparent and constructively critical assessment of its strengths and weaknesses, and lessons learned from the intervention. This debate will undoubtedly continue for some time. However, we are convinced that the decision to intervene was correct. We believe that intervention must send a clear message of our resolve to ensure that in the post-Cold War period, no military coups to overthrow democratically elected governments will be tolerated in our subregion.

The timely intervention which ended the mutiny and allowed the political process to progress prevented ever greater destabilisation, destruction and loss of life. Today an interim authority has been established. This is composed of two members each of the 12 political parties that contested the May elections. The task of this committee will be to create and promote conditions conducive to the holding of free and fair elections and levelling of the playing fields for all political parties and candidates. Its powers are wide-ranging and include a review of the Electoral Code of Conduct. A review of the Independent Electoral Commission and it will make recommendations on its structures and functions. The committee will also review the Lesotho Electoral System with a view to making it more democratic and representative. Recognition of the progress made by this body is seen in the recent withdrawal of South African military forces from Lesotho.

CONCLUSION

South Africa's Africa policy is one which is predicated on the principles which shaped our liberation and guide the international community, that is the promotion of peace, justice and equitable development. As South African policy makers face the many challenges to the continent on the eve of the twenty-first century, it is appropriate to consider the words of the venerated African statesmen Julius Nyerere:

As Africans we still have a great deal to contribute to the world. And our future cannot be determined without us. Either we acquiesce in a future determined for us by others or we seize control of it ourselves.

I am confident that South Africa will make a contribution to ensure that we Africans are determinants of our respective destinies. South Africa will seek to do this not in 'splendid isolation' but in co-operation with the world community of nations.

---

1   This chapter was written in November 1998 and reflects the situation at that time.

Chapter Five:

FRANCE'S AFRICAN POLICY IN TRANSITION: DISENGAGEMENT AND REDEPLOYMENT

Guy Martin

This chapter is an inquiry into the nature and substance of current French policy towards Africa. More specifically, it is an attempt to answer the following question: Is France's African policy truly in transition between old-style neocolonial and patrimonial type of policies characterised by intimate and quasi-familial relations between the French and francophone African elites – variously referred to as *le village franco-africain*,[1] or *la Françafrique*[2] – and a new policy in which francophone Africa is subsumed within a broader Third World policy thus becoming normalised (*normalisée* and *banalisée*)? In other words, is France resolutely moving away from its traditional policy of *domaine réservé* and *chasse gardée* towards a politico-diplomatic, military, economic and financial disengagement from and redeployment in Africa? In brief, are we truly witnessing a decolonisation of Franco-African relations?

A number of symbolic events clearly show that a new French African policy is currently taking shape, leading to a progressive divorce between France and francophone Africa. At the same time, built-in structural factors tend to favour a status quo policy. Thus, while some observers point to a genuine French disengagement and redeployment, others stress France's tendency to preserve the status quo. After an overview of the historical context and main characteristics of Franco-African relations, this chapter argues that France's African policy is truly at a transitional stage in which clear signs of change and new orientations coexist with old habits and status quo policies. It concludes that the extent to which real change will take place in Franco-African relations depends on the political will of the various actors involved, as well as on Africa's 'new leadership' tendency to exclude France and favor purely African solutions to African problems.

THE HISTORICAL CONTEXT AND MAIN CHARACTERISTICS OF FRANCO-AFRICAN RELATIONS[3]

In the aftermath of World War II, French policy makers initiated a process of decolonisation in Africa as they came to realise that the loss of formal control would not necessarily be accompanied by a loss of real power and influence on the continent. Shortly after assuming power as the first president of the Fifth French Republic (June 1958), General Charles de Gaulle translated his personal conception of *France-Afrique* into his project of a Franco-African community that would grant autonomy and internal government to the African colonies while France retained control over essential areas such as defence, foreign affairs, and economic, monetary, and strategic minerals policies. People throughout French Africa – except in Sékou Touré's Guinea – voted overwhelmingly in favour of the Franco-African community in the September 1958 referendum. However, the movement towards independence proved irresistible. Following the independence of the short-lived Mali Federation (Senegal and Mali) in June 1960, practically all former French African colonies became independent by August 1960. Thus the Franco-African community, as originally envisaged by de Gaulle, was stillborn.[4]

In fact, the independence of the African territories in 1960 was more the result of French goodwill and magnanimity than of the pressure of African nationalist movements. This peaceful transfer of power demonstrates that the francophone African elites overwhelmingly opted for a gradual process of decolonisation rather than a revolutionary break with the past; it also explains the emphasis placed on such values as moderation and compromise in the francophone African states' foreign policies. The transition from colonisation to *coopération* was smoothed before the formal granting of independence by the negotiation of comprehensive bilateral agreements between France and each francophone African state, covering such areas as defence and security; foreign policy and diplomatic consultation; economic, financial, commercial, and monetary matters; strategic minerals; and technical assistance. Through the linkage established between the accession to international sovereignty, the signing of model co-operation agreements, and the wholesale adoption of the French constitutional model of the Fifth Republic, France managed to institutionalise its political, economic, monetary, and cultural pre-eminence over its former African colonies, which thereby, and for the next three decades, remained excessively dependent on the motherland.

France's African policy: exclusivity, stability and continuity

France's African policy is characterised by exclusivity, stability and continuity. During the heyday of imperial expansion, France's economic dynamism and level of industrial development never quite matched that of its major European competitors (Britain and Germany). This explains why protectionism and autarchy were systematically applied to France's African empire and continued to shape its colonial and post-colonial policies. France's heavy reliance on explicit legal instruments is codified in the form of a highly normalised set of binding documents (the co-operation agreements), supported by a number of multilateral agencies (such as the franc zone and Franco-African summits). During the Cold War era, francophone Africa was perceived as belonging to the French sphere of influence by virtue of historical links and geographical proximity, and it was seen as constituting a natural French preserve (*domaine réservé*, or *pré-carré*), off limits to other foreign powers, whether friends (e.g. the US) or foes (e.g. the former Soviet Union). Indeed France has, on a number of occasions, shown a deep suspicion of the motives and actions of these power in Africa, as illustrated by the recent Franco-American rivalry in central and southern Africa, and in the Great Lakes region.[5]

Because they are based on historical links, geographical proximity, and linguistic and cultural affinity, relations between France and francophone Africa are particularly close and intimate, almost familial (*le village franco-africain*, or *La Françafrique*). And although family feuds may occasionally erupt, differences are never such that they cannot be quickly reconciled within the informal, warm, and friendly atmosphere of Franco-African institutions. This explains the extraordinary resilience and stability of Franco-African relations over the past four decades.

One of the most striking features of France's African policy is its continuity throughout the various political regimes of the Fifth French Republic, from 1958 to the present. There is no doubt that an autonomous and permanent policy exists, transcending the traditional political cleavages, the various regimes, and individual political leaders. The successive governments of Charles de Gaulle, Georges Pompidou, and Valéry Giscard d'Estaing have initiated and nurtured this African policy. In spite of his reformist intentions, François Mitterrand was left to manage, rather than to radically transform, this inheritance.[6] Paradoxically, the two periods of government cohabitation during which Mitterrand was forced to share power with a rightist parliamentary majority and prime minister (Jacques Chirac, 1986–88; Edouard Balladur, 1993–95) revealed the broad agreement that exists across party lines on the substance of France's African policy.

TOWARDS A NEW FRENCH POLICY IN AFRICA? SIX SYMBOLIC EVENTS

A new French African policy is currently being shaped by various symbolic events, leading to a Franco-African malaise. In a changing world environment characterised by the end of the Cold War and globalisation, French policy towards Africa is no longer determined by politico-diplomatic and geo-political factors, but by purely economic and financial considerations, namely the search for new African and Third World markets, and a renewed focus on European integration.

Six separate (though interrelated) events are symbolic of France's new African policy: the passing away of Houpouët-Boigny and Foccart; the La Baule doctrine; the Abidjan doctrine and the devaluation of the CFA franc; French setbacks in the Great Lakes region and the Zaire/Democratic Republic of the Congo/DRC *débacle*; the Franco-South African *rapprochement*; and French immigration policy. Each of these shall be briefly examined in turn.

The death of Houpouët-Boigny and Foccart: the end of an era?

The passing away of two key figures of the Franco-African family (*La Françafrique*), Félix Houpouët-Boigny (December 1993) and

Jacques Foccart (19 May 1997) truly signalled the end of an era in Franco-African relations. When he died in early December 1993, Félix Houpouët-Boigny had been president of Côte d'Ivoire since August 1960 and was unquestionably the doyen of francophone Africa and a key ally of France in the region. His close personal ties with several generations of French leaders were reflected in the level and size of the French delegation to his state funeral in Yamoussokro (February 1994), which included the late President Mitterand, then Prime Minister Balladur, former president Giscard d'Estaing, six former prime ministers, and more than 70 other dignitaries. As the *New York Times* envoy then remarked, 'Houpouët-Boigny's death is not only the end of a political era here, but perhaps as well the end of the close French-African relationship that he came to symbolize.'[7]

Jacques Foccart was the personal embodiment of continuity in Franco-African relations. A trusted adviser on African affairs and close confidante of the founder of the Fifth Republic, Charles de Gaulle, and of his successor, Georges Pompidou, Foccart was called back to duty by President Jacques Chirac in May 1995, and remained active until his death on 19 May 1997.

As he himself reveals in his memoirs, he carefully nurtured close personal (even familial) relations with the francophone African élite, and through a closely-knit network of public, private and occult individuals, organisations and interests (*les réseaux*), single-handedly managed to determine and control France's African policy in what he perceived to be France's best interest.[8] Interestingly, a close associate of Foccart, Fernand Wibaux has since 1995 retained an office at 14, rue de l'Elysée, which duplicates that of the 'official' adviser to the presidency on African affairs located at 2, rue de l'Elysée (Michel Dupuch).

The La Baule doctrine

In the early 1990s, France observed with some trepidation a process of democratisation – which it had not anticipated and over which it had no control – unfold in its former African colonies. However, France soon realised the inevitability of that process and promptly initiated a policy of political conditionality that established an explicit linkage between the provision of economic and financial assistance and the adoption of political reforms leading to liberal, multi-party democracy. Thus, at the June 1990 Franco-African summit meeting of La Baule in western France, the late President

Mitterand stressed the link between democracy and development and declared that 'French aid will be lukewarm towards authoritarian regimes and more enthusiastic for those initiating a democratic transition.'[9] However, a review of the evidence suggests that official pronouncements have not been followed by appropriate policy measures, and that France has continued steadfastly to support its authoritarian and corrupt friends in Africa.[10]

The Abidjan doctrine and the devaluation of the CFA franc

Formally adopted in January 1994, the 'Abidjan doctrine' states that henceforth French economic aid and financial assistance to the francophone African states is conditional upon the conclusion of stand-by agreements between the latter and the international financial institutions (IFIs: International Monetary Fund and World Bank). Similarly, the 50 per cent devaluation of the CFA franc on 12 January 1994, which signalled the demise of the Franco-African preferential monetary and trading area known as *la zone franc*, fell within the same strategy of de-linking between France and francophone Africa. Indeed, as Albert Bourgi cogently remarked at the time, 'the devaluation of the CFA franc will ultimately have a cathartic effect, that of mentally decolonizing the African leaders in their relations with France, thus finally cutting the umbilical cord which, for more than three decades, has tied them to their former metropole.'[11] In a recent study, Philippe Hugon argues that a degree of Franco-African monetary co-operation will subsist in spite of the fact that the CFA franc has, since January 1999, been formally linked to the euro in the context of the European monetary integration process to be completed by January 2002.[12] The reality is that in a context of increasing globalisation of the world economy, of relative French economic decline, and of deeper and broader European integration, France no longer has the financial wherewithal and political will to pursue an autonomous African policy distinct from that of its western partners. Hence the increasing multilateralisation of French official development assistance (ODA) through the IFIs and the European Union's European Development Fund (EDF).

French policy setbacks in the Great Lakes Region

From the October 1990 military intervention to rescue the Habyarimana regime to the *Opération Turquoise* (14 June–21 August 1994) designed to allow the *forces armées rwandaises* (FAR) to retreat into eastern Zaire, it has now been established that France provided continued diplomatic, military, technical and financial support to the *génocidaires* extremists of the Hutu Power (*Interahamwe* and FAR) who, in April 1994, planned and executed the genocide of some 850 000 Tutsis and moderate Hutus in Rwanda. As François-Xavier Verschave has noted, 'In Rwanda, France has backed a racist regime intent upon moving towards a 'final solution'. As acknowledged in the final report of the French Parliamentary Information Committee on Rwanda [*Mission d'information parlementaire française sur le Rwanda*] published on 15 December 1998, France largely contributed to financing, training and arming the military and security units which later executed the genocide.'[13] Jean-François Bayart has pointed put that this has considerably tarnished French prestige in Africa: 'Having been unable to prevent the RPF's [Rwanda Patriotic Front] victory, France became alienated from one of the major regional actors who later played a key role in the Zaïre/DRC crisis, discredited itself as an honest broker in the region and found itself compromised in the genocide. The resulting net loss of influence is enormous.'[14] The replacement of Mobutu Sese Seko's Zaïre, which France supported until the bitter end, by Laurent-Désiré Kabila's Democratic Republic of the Congo, supported by Rwanda's Kagame and Uganda's Museveni, on 17 May 1997 further aggravated French loss of influence in the subregion and exacerbated France's 'Fachoda syndrome' of an Anglo-Saxon plot to evict it permanently from its central African *chasse gardée*.[15] The fact that France proved unable to put together a coalition for a 'humanitarian' intervention in eastern Zaire in late 1996, the fall of Mobutu two months after Foccart's death and France's impotence in the face of the upheaval in early June 1997 in Brazzaville (where French troops simply evacuated French nationals) were all symptomatic of a major loss of French power and influence in central Africa.

France and South Africa: towards a new engagement in Africa?

Coming in the wake of French Foreign Affairs Minister Hubert Védrine's one-day visit to Cape Town (9 October 1997), French President Jacques Chirac's state visit to South Africa (26–28 June 1998) and other southern African countries (Angola, Mozambique and Namibia) was meant to demonstrate France's resolve in opening a new chapter in Franco-African relations while resolutely turning a page in the neocolonial relations that have traditionally characterised its relations with its former colonies in Africa. As France progressively disengages politically, economically and militarily from francophone sub-Saharan Africa, it can only view favourably South Africa's parallel involvement in France's former *domaine réservé*. Thus, South Africa's diplomatic involvement in the final stages of the DRC/Zaïre crisis, South African firms' active involvement in gold mining in countries such as Burkina Faso, Guinea, Mali and Niger, or South African farmers' new northern trek to Congo-Brazzaville or the DRC which would have never been allowed by *La Françafrique* are now tolerated (if not actively encouraged) by France. In search of new trading partners and new outlets for both public and private investments in Africa, France increasingly looks to South Africa as an ideal intermediary and power-broker to penetrate southern African markets which have for many years been firmly situated within South Africa's traditional sphere of influence.

With the end of apartheid, economic relations between France and South Africa have progressed steadily. Thus in 1997, the sale of French goods on the South African market increased by more than 27 per cent in real terms compared to 1996, reaching a record US $1 billion in value. South Africa has since then become France's main trading partner in sub-Saharan Africa, before Côte d'Ivoire and Nigeria. Altogether, the French market share in South Africa has increased to nearly 3 billion rand since 1994. Over 125 French firms now have a subsidiary in South Africa (a threefold increase since 1993). In 1997, French development aid to South Africa amounted to 230 million francs, and French cultural, educational and scientific aid (governed by a special protocol since February 1995) reached 42 million francs.[16] Following the visit to South Africa of French foreign affairs minister Hubert Védrine, a formal agreement setting up a Franco-South African Forum for Political Dialogue, conceived as a permanent mechanism for consultation in international affairs, was concluded between the two governments on 9 October 1997. Other signs of Franco-South African rapprochement include Vice-President Thabo Mbeki's participation in the 20th Franco-African summit meeting in Paris (26–28 November 1998); the inclusion of South Africa in France's newly defined *Zone de solidarité prioritaire* for purposes of French aid; and France's allocation of FF 3,5 million to SADC's Blue Crane war games conducted in April 1999 in South Africa. Thus while officially South Africa would prefer, for historical and political reasons, not to be seen as too closely associated with France, considerations of realpolitik dictate that it agrees to a marriage of convenience with France while the latter acknowledges the former's status as an ascending subregional power with budding continental ambitions, as evidenced by its vocal advocacy and active promotion of a pan-African policy of African renaissance.

French immigration policy

During the cohabitation régime in which a socialist president (François Mitterand) coexisted with a rightist government (with Charles Pasqua as Minister of Home Affairs) – between 1986 and 1988, and between 1993 and 1995 – France enacted extremely restrictive immigration policies specifically targetting francophone Africans (including *Maghrébins* from north Africa). Taking various despicable forms – the drastic reduction in the delivery of entry visas in France; a multiplicity of administrative obstacles and extreme bureaucratisation of the visa issuance process; the forced expulsion on charter planes of 'illegal' immigrants in degrading conditions; the forced expulsion of the African protesters at *Église Saint-Bernard* of Paris – this policy succeeded in antagonising many francophone Africans (including students, businessmen and politicians) and further contributed to a significant degradation of France's image in Africa. This led some observers to remark that France actively promoted a policy of *francophonie* while at the same time busily engaged in chasing the francophones away from France.[17]

HOW 'NEW' IS FRANCE'S NEW AFRICAN POLICY? BETWEEN A SECOND DECOLONISATION AND MAINTAINING THE STATUS QUO

Two opposing viewpoints of the evolving Franco-African relationship currently tend to prevail. According to the first view, we are now witnessing a real French disengagement from francophone Africa and a simultaneous redeployment of French politico-diplomatic, strategic and economic interests away from francophone Africa and into new territories in Africa (Nigeria, Angola, Namibia, Zimbabwe and South Africa) and other Third World countries (Brazil, India, Vietnam, etc.). The second view argues that this decolonisation policy is a mere smokescreen behind which the traditional status quo policy of *la Françafrique* is actually maintained. These two viewpoints shall be briefly examined below.

A new African policy of disengagement and redeployment: towards a second decolonisation?

While direct French presence had always been a hallmark of French co-operation policy in Africa, one observes a significant decrease in the number of both civilian and military technical assistants in Africa. Thus, the number of French civilian *coopérants* in Africa has decreased from 7 669 in 1988 to 2 919 in 1998, while that of their military counterparts has decreased from 954 to 570 during the same period.[18] This trend clearly indicates a move away from what the French call a *coopération de substitution* (aid substituting for local manpower) to a medium to long-term, project-based type of assistance.

Its renewed European focus, its economic and financial crisis, and setbacks experienced in the Great Lakes region have led France to reassess its security policy in Africa completely. This new French security policy in Africa is characterised by military disengagement (from 8 000 to 5 600 troops over the period 1997–2002); concentration of these troops in only five locations (Abidjan, Dakar, Djibouti, Libreville and N'Djamena) and the closure of two bases (Bangui and Bouar in the Central African Republic/CAR); financial, material and logistical support to subregional and pan-African peacekeeping forces (in co-operation with Britain and the US); and the relocation of military training from France to four subregional training centres in Africa (Thiès in Senegal; Koulikoro in Mali; and Bouaké in Côte d'Ivoire, where the Zambakro subregional peacekeeping training centre was inaugurated on 7 June 1999).[19]

A distinct French disengagement from Africa is taking place at the economic and financial levels as well. Following the general trend of 'donor fatigue', French ODA has decreased from FF 42,1 billion in 1995 to FF 34,7 billion in 1998, while the budget of the Ministry of Co-operation was reduced from FF 8 billion in 1993 to FF 6.4 billion in 1998.[20] Following the above Abidjan doctrine of 1994, this French disengagement has also taken the form of a gradual process of multilateralisation of French ODA whereby the provision of French aid to francophone African states is henceforth made conditional on the conclusion of agreements between the latter and the IFIs. Clearly, France no longer has the means to pursue an ambitious African policy.

Defending La Françafrique and maintaining the status quo

At the official level, various recent pronouncements by key *décideurs* of France's African policy (notably President Chirac and Foreign Minister Védrine) tend to indicate clearly that France does not intend to change its African policy, let alone to disengage from Africa, and that it remains faithful to its traditional African allies. As for the observable signs of change, they are rationalised as being a mere adaptation to changing circumstances.[21] Looking beyond the official discourse emphasising continuity in Franco-African relations within the *longue durée*, one may observe the survival of certain attitudes and of various individuals, networks, firms and institutions that have a vested interest in preserving *la Françafrique* for a few more years. These would include a cross-section of the French political and military elite; the *cellule africaine* at the *Elysee Palace*, manned by two *Foccartiens* (Michel Dupuch and Fernand Wibaux); the French oil major *Elf Aquitaine* (recently bought by *Total-Fina*) which for years has conducted its own autonomous African policy in its central African *chasses gardées* (notably Gabon and the Congo); the francophone African political and military elite from the core countries of *Françafrique* (Cameroon, Chad, Côte d'Ivoire, Gabon, Senegal, and Togo), linked to their French counterparts through various official and occult networks, such as the Freemasons;[22] various firms, experts and consultants who benefit from French ODA; and some non-governmental organisations benefitting from the provision of humanitarian assistance to Africa.

The brief exposé of these two conflicting perspectives actually points to a defining moment in Franco-African relations. What the preceding overview seems to indicate is that France's African policy has indeed entered a *transitional phase* in which clear signs of change coexist with status quo policies. Thus, while the edifice shows some cracks, it still stands. As we review the concrete manifestations of France's 'new' policy in Africa below, we must keep in mind the fact that in the grey areas of policy, new orientations may very well coexist with old habits for some time.[23]

How 'new' is the new French African policy?
Plus ça change, plus c'est la même chose ...

What is really 'new' in France's African policy? Not much, as a closer examination of that policy reveals.

a. *French military and security policy in Africa*

The restructuring of the French military announced in mid-1997 which resulted in the reduction and redeployment of French forces in Africa is, in fact, the logical outcome of a strategy of intervention from bases located in France (through a 44 500-men strong *Force d'action rapide*/FAR) as opposed to a strategy of direct military presence which was initiated in the late seventies. Thus, while the actual number of troops based in Africa is being reduced (from 8 000 to 5 600 between 1997 and 2002), their capacity to intervene will be maintained and even improved. Furthermore, as Albert Bourgi rightly observes, 'In spite of the reforms undertaken, French military presence in Africa retains a colonial character, as demonstrated by the decision to maintain bases in countries considered as strategic for the perpetuation of French political, economic and strategic influence on the continent, namely Senegal, Côte d'Ivoire, Gabon and Chad.' And he adds: 'French military presence in Africa appears more than ever as the symbol of an outdated imperial policy which is meaningless in the post-Cold War world ...'[24]

In the same way, one can view the new French policy of assistance to multinational and subregional peacekeeping forces in Africa in the context of continuity in French military policy in Africa. Thus, the *Mission interafricaine de stabilisation à Bangui* (MISAB), set up by France in the CAR in the spring of 1997, while made up of African contingents, has been armed, equipped, trained and managed by France. Similarly, the new French military policy of RECAMP *(Renforcement des capacités africaines de maintien de la paix)* was tested during the *Guidimakha* inter-African military war games conducted in Senegal in early 1998, which benefitted from significant technical, logistical and financial support from France, as well as from symbolic assistance from the US and Great Britain. Thus, in spite of an official French military policy of disengagement and redeployment, African technical, logistical and financial military dependency on France persists

b. *The management of the 1997 crisis in Congo-Brazzaville*

Throughout the civil war in Congo-Brazzaville in which the forces of the incumbent President Pascal Lissouba opposed those of former president Denis Sassou-Nguesso (June–October 1997), France officially maintained an attitude of strict 'neutrality' avoiding any military intervention (except for the evacuation of French nationals in June 1997) and actively supporting the mediation effort initiated by President Omar Bongo of Gabon. However, in this case, French official neutrality was quickly superseded by the 'benevolent neutrality' of the French state, notably the military establishment, the *Elysée* Palace and *Elf Aquitaine*, all of which, in effect, actively supported Sassou-Nguesso, who fought his way back into power on 25 October 1997 with the assistance of Chadian troops backed by French logistical support. *Elf* appears to have been the common denominator of the assistance which Sassou-Nguesso got from Angola and Gabon in his re-conquest of power. Indeed, in the spring of 1998, *elf* agreed to provide him with $310 million as the cost of the re-scheduling of the Congo's debt. President Chirac continues to support is old friend, Sassou-Nguesso, and General Jeannou Lacaze, former Chief-of-Staff of Mitterand and Mobutu, now serves as adviser to the Congolese army.[25] The management of the Congolese crisis clearly reveals a tension between the *anciens'* policy of 'benevolent neutrality' (in fact, of active support), and the *modernes'* official posture of non-interference and strict neutrality (as advocated by Prime Minister Lionel Jospin).

c. *France's 'non-intervention' in the 24 December 1999 military coup d état in Côte d'Ivoire*

On 24 December 1999, General Robert Guei took power in a bloodless military *coup d'état* which toppled the authoritarian and unpopular regime of Houpouët-Boigny's political heir, Henri Konan Bédié. The latter ended up in France on 3 January 2000, after having been whisked to safety under French military escort to Lomé, Togo. As Bédié left, 300 French paratroopers stood by in Dakar (Senegal) to enter Côte d'Ivoire in the name of protecting the 22 000 French nationals there, but were dissuaded by General Guei's warning that sending in French reinforcements would be unwise under the circumstances. France's 'sober' reaction to the coup in Côte d'Ivoire must be viewed in the context of the new

European Union's co-ordinated foreign policy under which France's bilateral African policy must henceforth be subsumed. French Co-operation Minister, Charles Josselin, indicated that France's approach to the coup reflected a 'new policy' of non-intervention in Africa. As he put it, 'We will no longer intervene in internal political debates. Maintaining a leader against the people's will is out of the question. What has happened in Côte d'Ivoire reflects France's new policy in Africa.'[26] Similar feelings were expressed by French Minister of Foreign Affairs, Hubert Védrine, when he remarked that 'Disengagement from Africa is not on the agenda; nor is intervention in internal conflicts, which now belongs to a bygone era,' adding: 'This being said, we remain firmly opposed to any forcible removal of a legitimate government.' Thus, according to him, France's main objective is to 'arrive promptly at an electoral timetable leading to a return to democracy and the rule of law.' In order to encourage this process, France has threatened to get the European Union's economic and financial assistance to Côte d'Ivoire suspended.[27] Indeed, the fact that the French government might simply be making a virtue out of a necessity seems to be confirmed by its 11 January decision to partially suspend its military co-operation with Côte d'Ivoire by asking 16 of its 37 technical military assistants posted there to stop working.[28]

This episode perfectly illustrates the fact that French African policy is progressively moving out of the exclusive domain (*domaine réservé*) of the presidency (*L'Elysée*) and into an area of increasingly shared responsibility with the prime minister's office (*Matignon*) and the government, to the advantage of the latter. The management of the Ivoirian crisis clearly shows that *Matignon* and the government, in the person of Prime Minister Lionel Jospin and Foreign Minister Hubert Védrine, were definitely opposed to any intervention to help Henri Konan Bédié stay in power, while the *Elisée*, particularly President Jacques Chirac and his African affairs adviser Michel Dupuch, a former ambassador to Abidjan, clearly wanted to rescue him under the usual pretence of the protection of French nationals. In the event, the *modernes* went through the motions of sending to Abidjan two helicopters and 40 men from the French military base at Libreville, Gabon and of prepositioning 300 *légionnaires* of the 2nd REP in Dakar, Senegal, but firmly resisted the *Elysée*'s (*anciens*) pressure to actually send these helicopters and troops into Côte d'Ivoire to rescue the beleaguered Bédié, who had urged the Ivoirian people to rise against the insurgents on *Radio France*

Internationale. As Foreign Minister Hubert Védrine remarked on this occasion, 'The Bédié case clearly demonstrates that France is now friendly without being complacent. Even our closest associates no longer have *carte blanche* (...) Our new policy is now firmly set between 'interventionism' and 'withdrawal.''[29]

d. *The reform of the French co-operation system*

Initiated by Prime Minister Lionel Jospin in February 1998 with the full backing of the *Elysée*, the reform of the French co-operation system is an attempt to adapt aging institutions to a changing world environment characterised by globalisation and the multilateralisation of ODA. The former Secretariat of State for co-operation has become a unit within the Ministry of Foreign Affairs (*le Quai d'Orsay*). Henceforth, the minister of foreign affairs will be responsible for all aspects of France's external relations. The new system revolves around two pillars: the *Quai d'Orsay* and *Bercy* (the Ministry of Economy and Finance), which jointly will supervise a new structure, the *Comité interministériel de la Coopération internationale et du développement* (CICID). The CICID will determine the co-operation policy and its geographical priorities. The renamed *Agence française de développement* (AFD) will have overall responsibility for the management and disbursement of French ODA. In order to maintain a degree of consistency between French ODA and unofficial assistance, a *Haut Conseil de la Coopération Internationale* (HCCI) with consultative status, which brings together representatives of NGOs, municipalities, academia, researchers and experts, has been set up. Henceforth, the main target of French ODA is a 'solidarity priority area' (*Zone de solidarité prioritaire*: ZSP) made up of the least developed countries falling within the purview of the Deputy-ministry of Co-operation (basically all the African, Caribbean and Pacific states signatories of the Lomé Convention, plus South Africa).

In the final analysis, does this structural reform represent a substantive change in France's co-operation policy? For some observers, this reform is merely an administrative rationalisation rather than a structural transformation. Thus, President Bongo of Gabon alluded to a mere semantic change when he remarked: 'I don't care whether you call the person in charge of co-operation minister, secretary or messenger; what matters is that the co-operation policy is maintained.'[30] Indeed, the *Elysée* maintains its *cellule africaine*; the military co-operation agreements are still in force; the ZSP includes all the 36 countries of the former *domaine réservé* (*pays du champ*); and Deputy-Minister of Co-operation, Charles Josselin, takes part in cabinet meetings, which constitutes a real advantage in the eyes of the francophone African heads of state. Ultimately, this reform perfectly illustrates the transitory nature of France's African policy.

CONCLUSION

This chapter has shown that France's African policy is currently in a transitional phase in which clear signs of change and new orientations coexist with old habits and status quo policies.

The growing influence of the French Socialist Party (PS) in determining France's African policy is symptomatic of this transitional phase. It is interesting to note in this regard that the *Monsieur Afrique* of the PS, Guy Labertit, who travels frequently to francophone Africa and entertains good relations with all major opposition leaders there, reports both to Prime Minister Lionel Jospin and to Deputy Minister for Co-operation, Charles Josselin, with whom he meets every two months.[31]

Ultimately, the extent to which real change will take place in Franco-African relations depends on two main factors. The first is a genuine political will for change among the main players involved: the French and African political, military and business elites; representatives of key NGOs; and French and African citizen's organisations. The second factor is the increasing tendency of Africa's 'new leadership', such as Uganda's Yoweri Museveni and Rwanda's Paul Kagame, to reject French presence and intervention in Africa, particularly in central Africa and the Great Lakes region, in favour of purely African solutions to African problems within appropriate regional (e.g. Organization of African Unity/OAU) or subregional (e.g. Southern African Development Community/SADC) institutional frameworks. Almost 40 years after independence, the time has really come for Africa's 'second decolonisation' to take place and for Franco-African relations to be truly decolonised. As eloquently stated by the CFA coalition (*coalition Citoyens France Afrique*), 'what we do not want is an African policy devoid of any democratic control and focused on short-term political and economic interests (...) African democratic aspirations must become a key component of renovated Franco-African and Euro-African relations built on the principles of equity and reciprocity.'[32]

1   See Antoine Glaser & Stephen Smith, *Ces messieurs Afrique 1: Le Paris-village du continent noir* (Paris: Calmann-Lévy, 1992); and A. Glaser & S. Smith, *Ces messieurs Afrique 2: Des réseaux aux lobbies* (Paris: Calmann-Lévy, 1997).
2   François-Xavier Verschave, *La Françafrique: le plus long scandale de la République* (Paris: Stock, 1998). The term of *Françafrique* has now gained wide currency through frequent usage, notably in the *Dossiers noirs de la politique africaine de la France* published at regular intervals by the French non-governmental organisation advocating a new African policy, Agir ici-Survie.
3   This section draws heavily on my earlier work: Guy Martin, 'Francophone Africa in the Context of Franco-African Relations,' in John W. Harbeson & Donald Rotchild (eds.), *Africa in World Politics: Post-Cold War Challenges* (Boulder, CO: Westview Press, 2nd edn., 1995), pp 163–188 (166–9 for this particular section).
4   See Patrick Manning, *Francophone Sub-Saharan Africa 1880–1995* (New York: Cambridge University Press, 2nd edn., 1998), pp 133–179; Keith Panter-Brick, 'Independence, French Style,' in Prosser Gifford & Wm. Roger Louis (eds.), *Decolonization and African Independence: The Transfer of Power, 1950–1980* (New Haven: Yale University Press, 1988), pp 73–104; Claude Wauthier, *Quatre Présidents et l'Afrique: de Gaulle, Pompidou, Giscard d'Estaing, Mitterand* (Paris: Éditions du Seuil, 1995), part I: 'Charles de Gaulle,' pp 17–179.
5   On Franco-American rivalry in Africa, see in particular Peter J. Schraeder, 'France and the Great Game in Africa,' *Current History* (May 1997), pp 210–1; P.J. Schraeder, 'The U.S. and France in Africa: Competition or Collaboration?' Paper presented at the 42nd annual meeting of the African Studies Association, Philadelphia, PA (11–14 November 1999).
6   See Claude Wauthier, op. cit. See also Jean-François Bayart, *La politique africaine de François Mitterand* (Paris: Karthala, 1984), who asserts that 'The real continuity actually starts with Mr. Mitterand [when he was minister for Overseas France in 1954] and was passed on to General de Gaulle and to his successors' (p. 52).
7   Kenneth B. Noble, 'Ivory Coast Buries its Father of Freedom,' *The New York Times* (8 February 1994), pp A1, A5.
8   Philippe Gaillard (entretiens avec), *Foccart Parle* (Paris: Fayard/Jeune Afrique); vol. 1 (1995); vol. 2 (1997); Jacques Foccart, *Tous les soirs avec de Gaulle* 1 (Paris: Fayard, 1997). For a concise and informative overview of Foccart's role and legacy in *Françafrique*, see Kaye Whiteman, 'The Man Who Ran Françafrique,' *The National Interest* no. 49 (Fall 1997), pp 92–99. For another perspective on Foccart , see Pierre Péan, *L'Homme de l'Ombre* (Paris: Fayard, 1990).
9   Quoted in Christian Casteran & Hugo Sada, 'Sommet de la Baule: l'avertissement,' in *Jeune Afrique* (27 June–3 July 1990), p. 15 [translated from the French by the author, as elsewhere in this paper].
10 These would include Rwanda's Juvénal Habyarimana and Zaïre's Mobutu Sese Seko until their demise and death; Cameroon's Paul Biya; Chad's Idriss Déby; Côte d'Ivoire's Henri Konan Bédié, Gabon's Omar Bongo and Togo's Gnassingbé Éyadéma.
11 Albert Bourgi, 'Dévaluation, emancipation ...' *Jeune Afrique* (20–26 January 1994), pp 46–7.
12 Philippe Hugon, *La zone franc à l'heure de l'euro* (Paris: Karthala, 1999), pp 219–228.
13 François-Xavier Verschave, *Complicité de génocide? La politique de la France au Rwanda* (Paris: La Découverte, 1994), p. 7; see also Agir ici-Survie, 'Rwanda: la France choisit le camp du génocide,' [Dossiers noir de la politique africaine de la France no. 1] (Paris: L'Harmattan, 1995), pp 7–64; Agir ici-Survie, *La sécurite au sommet, l'insécurité à la base* [Dossiers noirs de la politique africaine de la France no. 12] (Paris: L'Harmattan, 1998), pp 121–142. On the genocide, see Colette Braeckman, *Rwanda: histoire d'un génocide* (Paris: Fayard, 1994); and Gérard Prunier, *The Rwanda Crisis: History of a Genocide* (New York: Columbia University Press, 1995). On *Opération Turquoise*, see G. Prunier, op. cit, pp 281–311. Agir ici-Survie reveals that as early as 1992, the French state bank *Crédit Lyonnais* acted as collateral for a $6 million Rwandan arms purchase from Egypt and that on the day following the outbreak of the genocide (8 April 1994), a heavily armed French brigade (*Amaryllis*) landed in Kigali, one of its planes carrying ammunition for the FAR (Agir ici-Survie, Dossiers noirs no. 12, op. cit., pp 206–7). See also: *Rapport de la Mission d?information parlementaire française sur le Rwanda*, 15 décembre 1998 [Pierre Brana & Bernard Cazenave, Rapporteurs].
14 Jean-François Bayart, '*Bis repetita*: La politique africaine de François Mitterrand de 1989 à 1995,' Colloque sur *La politique extérieure de François Mitterrand à l'épreuve de l'après-guerre froide*, Centre d'études et de recherches internationales (CERI), Paris (13–15 May 1997), p. 20.

15 On recent developments in central Africa, see Colette Braeckman, *L'Enjeu Congolais: L'Afrique centrale après Mobutu* (Paris: Fayard, 1999).
16 Economic and financial data provided by the Economic & Trade Development Office [*Poste d'expansion économique*], French Embassy in South Africa, Pretoria (May 1998).
17 Mentioned in Philippe Marchesin, 'La politique africaine de la France en transition,' *Politique africaine* no. 71 (October 1998), pp 93–4.
18 Data provided in the French National Assembly Parliamentary Financial Committee's Report on Foreign Affairs and co-operation for 1998 [A. Adevah-Poeuf, rapporteur], quoted in P. Marchesin, *art. cit.*, p. 97.
19 See Jean-Dominique Geslin, 'Quels gendarmes pour l'Afrique?' *Jeune Afrique* (15–21 June 1999), pp 27–8, which notes that the Zambakro training centre is financed by France to the tune of 15 million francs.
20 French National Assembly, *Adevah-Poeuf Report*, 1998, pp 9, 23; P. Marchesin, 'L'aide publique au développement en 1997,' *Observatoire permanent de la coopération française*, Rapport 1997 (Paris: Karthala, 1997), p. 17.
21 For a representative sample of such French official pronouncements, see P. Marchesin, 'La politique africaine de la France en transition,' op. cit., pp 99–100.
22 On the resilience of Franco-African Freemason networks in Africa, see in particular Claude Wauthier, 'L'étrange influence des francs-maçons en Afrique francophone,' *Le Monde diplomatique* (September 1997), pp 6–7.
23 This point is eloquently made by P. Marchesin, 'La politique africaine de la France en transition,' op. cit., p. 101.
24 Albert Bourgi, 'La fin de l'épopée coloniale?' *Jeune Afrique* (13–26 August 1997); A. Bourgi, 'Centrafrique: la tentation impériale.' *Jeune Afrique* (15–21 January 1997), p. 15.
25 See Agir ici-Survie, *La Sécurité au Sommet, l'insécurité à la base* [Dossiers noirs de la politique africaine de la France no. 12] (Paris: L'Harmattan, 1998), pp 81–112.
26 Quoted in Ruth Nabakwe, 'Ivory Coast: Lessons from Africa's latest coup d'etat,' *Panafrican News Agency* (30 December 1999).
27 All the quotes are from Vincent Hugeux, 'La France et le test ivoirien,' *L'Express* (30 décembre 1999).
28 Since its independence from France in August 1960, Côte d'Ivoire and its former President, Félix Houpouët-Boigny have traditionally been considered a core country and key ally in terms of French presence and policy in Africa. The French expatriate community numbers 22 000 in all, with 300 French firms operating there. In addition to the 37 French technical military assistants, another 200 French civilian technical assistants are posted there. In 1998, 51 Ivoirian military officers underwent advanced training in various French military academies. As a result of the recent redeployment of French military personnel and bases in Africa, 550 French troops [43rd *bataillon d'infanterie de marine*] remain stationed at Port-Bouët, a base adjacent to Abidjan's international airport from which former President Henri Konan-Bédié was whisked to safety from the French ambassador's residence to Lomé, Togo (figures from *Radio France Internationale/ MFI*, 'Afrique/France: Les habits neufs de la coopération militaire,' No. 931 (30 October 1998); 'Afrique/France: La France recentre son engagement africain sur le maintien de la paix,' No. 967 (9 November 1998); and V. Hugeux, 'La France et le test ivoirien,' in op. cit.
29 This situation is chronicled in some detail in Stephen Smith, 'L'Elysée perd sa chasse en Afrique,' *Libération* (10 février 2000), which also includes Védrine's quote.
30 Quoted in Philippe Gaillard, 'Feu la 'Coopé',' in *Jeune Afrique* (10–16 February 1998), p. 9.
31 François Soudan, 'Les certitudes de Guy Labertit,' *Jeune Afrique* (7–13 décembre 1999), p. 24; see also F. Soudan, 'Le tour d'Afrique de Charles Josselin,' in *Ibidem*, pp 22–24.
32 Agir ici-Survie, *Jacques Chirac et la Françafrique. Retour à la case Foccart?* [Dossiers noirs de la politique africaine de la France no. 6] (Paris: L'Harmattan, 1995), pp 08, 111.

Chapter Six:

THE ECONOMIC RELATIONS OF FRANCE AND SOUTH AFRICA WITH AFRICA

Philippe Hugon[1]

France and South Africa have, historically, always maintained relations with Africa. Both have had their own areas of influence: France, with its preserve (*domaine réservé*) in the franc zone area, and South Africa in southern Africa, mainly with the member states of the South African Customs Union (SACU) and the South African Development Community (SADC). Today, the franc zone and the rand zone remain the only two regional monetary areas in Africa.

In the meantime, the national, regional and world contexts have changed considerably. France has progressively withdrawn economically from its former colonial empire and became more and more integrated with Europe and the world. Today, France has closer economic relations with major non-franc zone countries in Africa (such as Nigeria and South Africa) than with franc zone countries. South Africa, which had long been a protectionist country, has opened up its economy, integrated southern Africa, and negotiated a free trade agreement with the European Union while diversifying its foreign partners. This evolution is part of a process of internationalisation of the economy and of shifting centres of power leading to the economic marginalisation of sub-Saharan Africa.

GLOBALISATION OF THE ECONOMY

Since 1950, world trade has increased by slightly more than six per cent per year on average, multiplied by 14. In volume, world production has increased by just under four per cent (it was multiplied by 5,5) This increase, noticeable since 1990, is due to the liberalisation of financial transactions, to the technological revolution which has shrunk the world, and to the international strategies of the major economic groups. The majority of commercial transactions emanate from multinational firms (one-third of the total), and from international trade between subsidiary and parent companies (closed international trade). World trade is on the increase for commodities with a high added value and for services. Common primary products (commodities) which are traded on world markets (actual and futures markets) represented half of world trade in 1950, but represent only 20 per cent of such trade today. The stability of market prices depends largely on the economic situation prevailing in industrialised countries. Over the long term, market prices decreased in real terms by 50 per cent between 1970 and 1995. Conversely, products with high added value are traded on fragmented markets. Both the 'symbol manipulators' (Reich) and the service sector (production and individual-based) are becoming increasingly significant. Services (such as information, telecommunications, transport and tourism), which are now included in the World Trade Organization (WTO) agreements, represent 30 per cent of merchandise trade.

The increase in world trade is mainly due to intra-Triad trade (i.e. trade between Western Europe, North America and East Asia). The vertical international division of labour between countries with unequal development (a division which relates only to subsidiary commodities) has been replaced by a horizontal division of labour between countries with comparable levels of development (a division which relates only to commodities). The North still accounts for two-thirds of world trade. The African countries specialising in primary products are confined in their role as primary producers as world demand for their products decreases and competition increases.

The bulk of direct investment flows takes place among OECD countries. However, before the East Asian crisis of July 1997, a reorientation of the flows towards emerging markets was taking place. Direct investment in developing countries increased from US $18 billion in 1990 to almost US $100 billion in 1996, with 12 developing countries accounting for 80 per cent of these flows. The emerging

Asian financial markets represented about one-fourth of total direct investment. Direct investment in China increased from US $4,6 billion in 1980 to US $37 billion in 1995. Africa accounted for only US $12 billion of this investment in 1996.

Lastly, financial globalisation has led to turbulence. Between 1980 and 1993, the GNP of the OECD countries increased 2,5 times, the value of international trade by 3,4, that of financial assets on the major markets by 7,7, while financial transactions increased 15-fold. Transactions on foreign exchange markets reached US $1,2 billion per day, or 50 times more than actual commodity trade. Trading across borders for assets and bonds within the G7 went from 35 per cent of GDP in 1985 to 140 per cent 10 years later. Commercial banks are increasingly involved in transactions derived from private contracts (an estimated US $41 billion). Financial deals generate almost countless by-products. The increasingly sophisticated products negotiated are becoming standardised. There is a disjunction between real deals (trade and investment) and the financial sphere. Indirect financial integration via the euro market, which reflects an international economy based on credit, has given way to financing by the markets. Financial integration results from the mobility of capital and the fact that assets can be substituted (Bourguinat). African countries (with the exception of South Africa) have limited stock exchange investments and essentially receive a flow of public capital.

THE ECONOMIC MARGINALISATION OF AFRICA

Despite clear signs of recovery, Africa remains largely removed from worldwide financial dynamics and from the erratic movements which characterise them. Despite the implementation of liberalisation and open-door policies, Africa is increasingly marginalised in terms of commercial, technological and financial flows leading to a forced de-linking. The share of direct investment in Africa (as a percentage of total investment in less developed countries) decreased from six per cent in 1985 to four per cent in 1996. Thirty years ago, the average income in Africa represented 14 per cent of the income of developed countries, as opposed to seven per cent today. Africa then accounted for three per cent of world trade, as opposed to 1,3 per cent now. Nevertheless, a modest recovery of growth and private investment may be observed. These have doubled between 1994 and 1996, reaching US $12 billion. But this growth is mainly due to the

South African economy and to investment in the oil sector. Despite this increase, the African share of direct investment decreased from three per cent at the beginning of the 1990s to 2,3 per cent in 1996.

This chapter will describe the asymmetrical economic relations between France and South Africa with Africa; offer a theoretical explanation of these relations; and outline the prospects opened up by further European integration.

A comparison of asymmetrical economic relations

Relations between France and South Africa, on the one hand, and South Africa and Africa, on the other, are characterised by major asymmetries derived from colonialism. Yet while South Africa remains strongly integrated with southern Africa, France is progressively disengaging from its former colonial empire.

Trade relations between France and francophone Africa are extremely unequal. Thus, with a population 25 per cent greater than that of France, African countries from the franc zone account for only four per cent of France's GDP or only 1,5 per cent of its money supply. The share of the franc zone in French foreign trade dropped to 1,3 per cent in 1998, while France absorbed about one-fourth of the zone's exports.

In 1950, the colonial empire accounted for 60 per cent of French foreign trade. Imperial preferences resulted in the preservation of French interests in the quasi-monopolistic zone created by the 'Colonial Pact'. As an archaic form of capitalism, the colonial system was based on the articulation of merchant capital (backed by the colonial administration) with traditional or indigenous modes of production. The privileged relations between the metropole and its colonies partly reproduced the former 'Colonial Pact' – characterised by monopoly of the colonial state, diversion of financial flows toward the metropole, protectionism, and extra import-export duties. The colonies were sources of tropical produce and outlets for manufactured goods. This system was progressively transformed. After World War II, the colonial state became the main agent of development. The FIDES (*Fonds d'Investissement pour le Développement Économique et Social*) plan led to a sharp increase in public investment in the French colonies of Africa, thus encouraging private investment. Most of the modern sector of the economy, however, remained firmly in French hands. After independence, the successor state to the French colonial administration took over the commanding heights of the economy. The post-colonial state was mostly externally financed and relied on foreign trade. As for private African capital, it played only a minor role. This situation evolved gradually. The African economies were unable to avoid primary specialisation. Colonial interests in Africa have generally taken the form of rentier capitalism, inefficient and profitable only in specific sectors. The main beneficiaries of the system were import-export trading companies, commodities and mineral-producing firms and banks.

PRESERVING THE FRANC ZONE

Today, the franc zone is generally perceived by most observers as an area where French economic interests prevail, if not dominate. However, these interests are now fading away. Nevertheless, the franc zone remains characterised by unequal economic relations in terms of private capital flows, public investment and disbursement of official development assistance as private capital outflows exceed public capital inflows. The partial preservation of the interests of French firms can be observed. Thus, these firms continue to benefit from the use of a common currency, from the monetary co-operation mechanism, and from the French state's direct subsidies to the African states or firms operating in Africa. According to Jean-Pierre Prouteau (*Jeune Afrique*, 1994), a leading representative of French business interests in Africa, 'the franc zone consists of 80 firms, 1200 subsidiaries and 1000 small businesses or industries. The franc zone also represents a turnover of FF 100 billion.' Certain French firms benefit from rent situations derived from the 'trade economy' or the financial networks. Seventy per cent of the banking sector's turnover is produced by the three largest French banks (namely *Banque Nationale de Paris*, *Société Générale* and *Crédit Lyonnais*). A new form of capitalism has been able to take advantage of the privatisation and economic restructuring programmes. Linked French aid has resulted in contracts mostly benefitting French firms, notably construction and public works companies (such as Bouygues and Dumez). The most important French economic interests are found in the oil sector. Thus, the French state corporation, *Elf-Total*, has a dominant position in Central African oil-producing countries, particularly in Gabon and Congo-Brazzaville.

Nevertheless, one can observe a relative withdrawal of most French firms from Africa. Total direct French investment in the area amounts to FF 10 billion. In 1994, French trade (import/export) with non-franc zone countries – namely South Africa, Nigeria, Mauritius and Madagascar, valued at FF 22 billion – exceeded French trade with franc zone countries (Côte d'Ivoire, Cameroon, Gabon and Senegal, valued at FF 17 billion) (source: *Marchés Tropicaux*). French economic interests in non-franc zone African countries are essentially in the mining and oil sectors (Angola and Nigeria).

South Africa has recently become one of France's first African trading partners. In 1996, 14 per cent of France's imports from Africa came from South Africa (valued at FF 2,7 billion out of a total of 66 billion), and 9 per cent of its exports to Africa went to that country (valued at FF 46 billion out of 82 billion). While French firms are significantly involved in this partnership, the importance of public financial flows is limited: in 1997, less than half of French official development assistance (ODA) was earmarked for franc zone countries (FF2.2 billion), while FF 822 million was set aside for non-franc zone African countries (including FF 210 million for South Africa alone). Since July 1997, French foreign trade has been characterised by trade stability with Europe; an increase in exports to non-European OECD countries; a decrease in exports to Eastern Europe and Asia; and a noticeable redeployment towards Africa, despite the fall in oil prices. The trade balance with Africa has remained essentially positive, the continent absorbing about five per cent of French exports.

TOWARD A NORMALISATION OF FRANCO-AFRICAN RELATIONS WITHIN THE FRANC ZONE

The Abidjan doctrine enunciated by French Prime Minister Édouard Balladur in July 1993 and the devaluation of the CFA franc in January 1994 have drastically changed the rules of the game. Franc zone African countries lost their automatic drawing rights on the French treasury. Deferring to the Bretton Woods institutions, France has now become a 'residual' lender which intervenes only after multilateral agencies (such as the African Development Bank) have been mobilised. As a result, the relations of the franc zone countries with France have been normalised. France must allow these countries to regain their creditworthiness and to mobilise public and private bilateral (essentially European) aid. The elimination of the Ministry of Co-operation in 1998 reflects the normalisation of France's relations with its former African colonies and the end of special relationships and clientelism, even though defence agreements, a linguistic community, and economic interests subsist.

The debt burden and overdue reimbursements have helped transfer supervisory powers from France to the Bretton Woods institutions. The franc zone is no longer a private domain. The intervention of the World Bank or the European Union sometimes leads to conflict with France, as demonstrated by the case of the privatisation of cotton production in Sahel countries which affected the monopoly position of the French firm *Compagnie Française pour le Développement du Textile* (CFDT) *vis-à-vis* such upstarts as Cargill.

ECONOMIC RELATIONS OF SOUTH AFRICA WITH THE REST OF AFRICA

By any indicators, South Africa is the most powerful country in southern Africa. South Africa has long been (and continues to be) a dominant power in the integration process of southern Africa. Under the protectionist policies of the apartheid regime agreements between mining capital and the state, as well as the benefits of a protected market, were made possible by a fairly competitive South African export sector (Coussy, 1996). Industrialisation through import-substitution was financed by the large primary export sector which enabled the subsidisation of start-up industries and the diversification of economic activities. Regional integration was proceeding apace within the Southern African Customs Union (SACU) and the Common Monetary Area (CMA). Furthermore, regional integration was actually occurring through the major South African corporations. The SACU and CMA constituted highly integrated trade and monetary unions. South Africa's economic dominance of southern Africa was characterised by its large private sector, its elaborate transportation network, and its 700 000 migrant workers from southern Africa and their huge income transfers. The integration process within the Southern African Development Co-ordination Conference (SADCC) was rather ambiguous. During the 1970s and 1980s there was a shift in the relations of SADCC with South Africa owing to foreign aid. Most countries in southern Africa were affected by the South African destabilisation policy. Six of the 11 SADCC countries were landlocked, and six had common borders with South Africa. In the early 1980s, 90 per cent of the SADCC exports were using South African transport routes or ports. These countries became tightly integrated by the migration of workers and by intra-regional goods and capital flows. Foreign aid also enabled the SADCC countries to become more autonomous vis-à-vis South Africa. Thus, by the early 1990s, only half of SADCC trade still transited through South Africa.

The end of apartheid and liberalisation have had a profound impact on the regional integration process in general, and on intra-regional relations in particular. In August 1992, SADCC was changed into the Southern African Development Community (SADC). Immigration to South Africa, as well as trade between southern Africa and South Africa increased sharply. Official development assistance, as well as investment in regional mining, agri-business, and the transport sector also increased. South Africa joined SADC and negotiated several free trade agreements within the Indian Ocean region as well as with the European Union. South Africa also tried to revive former agreements with SADC member states. All this occurred within a context of foreign trade liberalisation and structural adjustment programmes in most southern African countries.

South Africa, which accounts for 44 per cent of SADC's population and three-fourths of SADC's production, could easily become the cornerstone of the community (SADC), but the forces of disintegration are currently stronger than those of integration. While economic relations with South Africa are vital for the southern African countries, the reverse is not true (except for the export of manufactured goods and investment in the mining sector). South Africa's foreign trade is mostly oriented towards Europe and, increasingly, towards East Asia and Latin America. The debate around the costs and benefits of integration within southern Africa pits the business community against the politicians.

Although – except for the SACU and CMA – southern Africa exhibits a moderate degree of institutional integration, South Africa plays an important integrating role within the subregion. Thus, intra-regional trade stands at about seven per cent of total foreign trade (Cassim, 1996). A distinction must be made between South African integration within southern Africa, the South African regional links outside the continent, and the current overlap between regional integration organisations of which South Africa is a member (e.g. SADC), and organisations of which South Africa is not a member (e.g. the Common Market for Eastern and Southern Africa/COMESA).

In 1980, a process of monetary, economic and political integration was initiated in 1980 around the SACU (free trade, common external tariff, common revenues and protected markets in exchange for financial transfers from South Africa to Botswana, Lesotho, Swaziland and Namibia). The SACU is based on intra-community protectionism and financial compensation for lost revenues provided by South Africa to the other member states which directly consume protected products. The rationale for, and functioning of, this customs union is now being reviewed in a context of new political relations in southern Africa, greater autonomy of southern African states vis-à-vis South Africa, liberalisation of foreign trade and the unwillingness of South Africa to continue to assume responsibility for financial compensation. Extending SACU membership to other southern African countries is not a viable option for several reasons. Firstly, tariff rates vary greatly between these countries. Secondly, the compensation mechanism has reached its limits.

The Common Monetary Area (CMA) has the same membership as the SACU (except for Botswana). The rand zone is, together with the franc zone, the only regional monetary union found in Africa. The rand is the currency used by the CMA member countries, and the South African Central Bank defines the monetary policies within the area. As is the case with the SACU, the rand zone is challenged by the greater autonomy of southern African countries vis-à-vis South Africa, and by these countries' progress towards monetary independence. In any event, the CMA does not constitute an appropriate model for a broader monetary union. Under the present circumstances, a monetary union is impossible or premature. A modest level of harmonisation of monetary policies only exists within SADC as a result of the implementation of IMF recommendations.

Whether measured in terms of 1995 GDP (US $118 billion vs US $33 billion) or external trade (US $48 billion vs US $24 billion), South Africa's share far exceeds that of the other eleven SADC member states combined (fourfold and double respectively). South Africa exports five times more to SADC countries than the latter export to South Africa. SADC has adopted a gradualist approach to regional integration. SADC's objective is to create a community based on peace and regional security, inter-sectoral co-operation and regional integration. South Africa advocates a step-by-step approach, taking into account the available natural and human resources (Department of Foreign Affairs, 1996). The Trade Protocol of May 1996 introduced several institutional reforms. The main objective was to transform the sectoral co-operation of SADCC into harmonised macro-economic policies and SADC industrial and transport co-operation projects. This is not only about an open-door, market-driven strategy, but about ambitious industrial policies. However, the member states' levels of economic development vary greatly. Malawi, Zambia and Zimbabwe are the countries with the highest percentage of intra-regional trade (40 per cent of imports). South Africa, which accounts for two-thirds of intra-SADC imports, realises only seven per cent of its exports and two per cent of its imports with SADC countries. A free trade agreement with SADC without a common external tariff could favour agri-industrial, chemical and mechanical South African industries, but would result in losses for imports of apparel, footwear and tobacco products from Zimbabwe. And while South Africa is the hub of a potential regional integration process, it does not want to become a 'substitute metropole': 'South Africa's rationale for joining SADC is essentially a political one, namely the need to reduce migratory pressures, fear of instability in neighbouring countries, jobcreation in the periphery, and the latter's need for capital. However, South Africa is not exactly ready to assume the financial obligations that such a leadership entails in terms of redistribution of activities, financial assistance or compensatory mechanisms for lost revenues' (Coussy, 1997:8).

THEORETICAL INTERPRETATIONS OF THESE ASYMMETRICAL RELATIONS

The persistence of economic relations of asymmetrical interdependence between South Africa and France with Africa may be analysed by resorting to new theories of multilateralism, regionalism and political economy which go beyond traditional heuristic theories of imperialism and dependency.

Tied transactions and multilateral approaches

Special relationships may be analysed from a liberal perspective which is promoted, *inter alia*, by the Bretton Woods institutions as neocolonial or protectionist, anti-market policies. Driven by these international financial institutions (IFIs), multilateral trade, financial liberalisation and the free circulation of goods and capital tend to reduce preferences and to open up the economies.

Most African countries (including South Africa) are currently implementing unilateral liberalisation policies with varying degrees of intensities and frequencies. These policies contradict past regional protectionism and raise problems of the compatibility of the economic policies of various countries. In countries like Zimbabwe, unilateral liberalisation has led to the de-industrialisation of the economy. For most southern African countries, unilateral liberalisation contradicts the principles of regionalism and trade and exchange rate rules among member states of SADC or COMESA. SACU-type customs unions and Lomé Convention-type preferential, non-reciprocal agreements contravene WTO regulations. Traditionally protectionist, South Africa is reluctant to eliminate all tariff barriers and to harmonise its policies with those of the most liberal SADC member states. Fundamentally, South Africa must choose between further integration with Europe through a free trade agreement or with southern Africa, where its industrial products have a comparative advantage.

The benefits of each of these trade policies may be assessed according to various criteria. A traditional criterion relates to static advantage in terms of welfare related to trade creation or trade diversion (e.g. models of partial equilibrium customs unions or models of general equilibrium). Another (institutional) criterion is that of the credibility and stability of policies. These considerably reduce the risks associated with uncertainty in trade policies for the various economic players and help attract capital flows. A third dynamic criterion is that related to the pace of economic reform, to building comparative advantage, and to the protection of sensitive sectors. Historical experience shows that industrialised countries (including those of South East Asia) have all, during their first phase of industrialisation, put in place selective protectionist policies which enabled them to build industries based on both import-substitution and export-promotion. It remains to be seen whether such a process remains valid in a context of globalisation and of export-oriented commercial strategies. A fourth criterion is that of the cost of transactions, of negotiations, of control of, and access to, information, and of external relations based on proximity and confidence.

FUTURE PROSPECTS FOR EUROPEAN EXTERNAL ECONOMIC RELATIONS

The European Union (EU) constitutes an integrated regional area with real clout in the world economy. It accounts for 27 per cent of world GDP, 37 per cent of world exports, 47 per cent of the world's direct investment, 23 per cent of world savings, 40 per cent of the world's bond market, 50 per cent of the world's money market and 20 per cent of the world's stock exchange transactions.

Impact of monetary integration

The euro became the official currency of most EU member states on 1 January 1999. It is expected to attract capital investment owing to the elements of trust, an integrated regional area and a credible monetary policy. However, a number of issues, such as the number of countries involved, the actual exchange rate on "D" day and the rate of exchange remain problematic. A strong euro would translate into low interest rates, but also low European commercial competitivity. The implementation of the Amsterdam or Maastricht Treaty will have a significant impact on the evolution of the franc zone. The Maastricht agreement provides for compatibility between the European single currency and the rules and regulations of the franc zone, notably with regard to the linkages between the CFA and Comoros francs to the French franc and the operation's accounts mechanism. Budgetary decisions remain a sovereign prerogative of states. However, monetary co-operation agreements are binding on the French treasury. The CFA franc/euro exchange rate will automatically be based on the CFA franc/French franc exchange rate (which is expected to remain unchanged) and on the French franc/euro exchange rate. The key variable, however, is that of the dollar/euro exchange rate. This is because African countries are competing with countries whose trade and financial transactions are mostly denominated in dollars.

African regional monetary unions should progressively increase their autonomy vis-à-vis the French treasury as a result of greater economic convergence and interdependence, and the implementation of co-ordinated and credible policies favouring market integration. The value of the single currency must reflect the state of the economic fundamentals at any given time. This progressive evolution should be managed in consultation with the non-franc zone African partners as well as with the European Union. All concerned should back monetary co-operation agreements between franc zone and non-franc zone African countries, as well as a possible enlargement of the rand zone. Monetary reform also raises strategic choices relating to the possible establishment of a preferential Euro-African area in a post-Lomé IV context.

THE FUTURE OF THE LOMÉ CONVENTION[2]

The EU-ACP [Africa, Caribbean & Pacific states] Lomé Convention is a neocolonial agreement based on regionally based preferential treatment and non-reciprocity. Duly taking into account the asymmetrical international relations, the Convention is made up of several, interrelated, components, namely a preferential trade agreement, financial and technical co-operation and institutional support.

The Lomé Convention, which expires on 29 February 2000, has, since its inception in 1975, progressively lost legitimacy and specificity. The current debate revolves around the geographical scope, the priority players and countries, and the sectors of co-operation needing particular attention in the successor agreement.

However, several studies show that the Lomé preferences have acted as a catalyst, and that they have led to trade expansion and diversification in certain countries such as Jamaica, Kenya, Mauritius and Zimbabwe. However, these preferences do not appear to have been sufficient (or even the necessary) substance. In this regard, three crucial factors must be taken into account.

Firstly, trade liberalisation has progressively eroded the generalised system of preferences. Secondly, Europe has been forced to manage the contradictions that emerged between maintaining a privileged relationship with geographically and historically close areas (Africa and the Mediterranean basin) and a new economic dynamic driving Europe outwards towards newly industrialising countries (particularly those of Asia). Since the fall of the Berlin wall, Europe's strategic centre has progressively moved eastwards. As a result, EU member states differ as to which geographical areas are to be given priority treatment. Aid to the ACP states, which accounted for 65 per cent of the EU's foreign aid under the 6th European Development Fund (EDF), had fallen to only 33,5 per cent of such financing under the 8th EDF. The main beneficiaries of this redeployment have been the PECO and Mediterranean countries. Lastly, since Lomé IV, the EU has accepted the rationale for structural adjustment. European financial assistance has focussed more on the macro-economic sector and is now quickly disbursed. Macro-economic support now far outweighs project aid. Thus, funds earmarked for Stabex, Sysmin and and the Structural Adjustment Facility accounted for over 30 per cent of total allocations under the 7th and 8th EDFs. As a result, the main focus is not on stabilising the economies of the ACP states, but on creating the conditions for their gradual integration into the world economy. Conditionalities have replaced partnership. Specific budgetary support is provided within the context of financial coherence and consistency. Structural adjustment has also led to a doctrinal convergence among the aid donors, under the leadership of the Bretton Woods institutions. Aid disbursement is made conditional upon satisfactory progress in negotiations between the ACP states and these institutions. This has resulted in a greater degree of co-ordination among donors in terms of structural adjustment policies and the management of local funds, but has also led to a loss of specificity of the original European aid policy. Grant aid has, however, contributed to preserve priority sectors and has resulted in significant net transfers, especially compared with those of the World Bank whose loans typically generate debt servicing.

In this regard, several possible scenarios may be envisaged:

- An **improved status quo** in which non-reciprocity, differential treatment, contractual agreements and priority market access would be maintained. The pluses of such a scenario would be to maintain a uniform framework and to take into account asymmetries. Its adoption would, however, require an exemption clause – most unlikely to be granted – with regard to articles XXV, 5 and IX of the WTO Treaty
- A **global agreement**, supplemented by bilateral agreements. A total integration of the ACP states within the Generalised System of Preferences (GSP) would result in the elimination of the trade provisions of the Lomé Convention, which would then be limited to a mere programme of financial assistance and which could include special preferences for the least-developed ACP states. This particular scenario, which would lead to harmonisation of policies among developing countries, conforms to WTO rules.
- Break-up of the Lomé Convention into separate **regional agreements** which would include regionally based free trade agreements. Following a transition period, the level of reciprocity might vary. This would require a multi-level management approach in terms of free trade areas and GSP.
- A **restructuring of the agreements** designed to benefit the least-developed ACP and non-ACP countries, irrespective of past colonial ties, on the basis of differential reciprocity. This

would entail the absorption of the Stabex and Sysmin mechanisms into a single financial co-operation protocol, as well as the elimination of the sugar, banana and meat protocols.

The European Union/South Africa free trade agreement[3]

The negotiations which led to the conclusion, in March 1999, of a Trade, Development and Co-operation Agreement between the EU and South Africa is often presented as a model post-Lomé agreement. Following the end of the apartheid era in April 1994, South Africa became, in April 1997, a qualified member of the Lomé Convention. The agreement – similar to that concluded between the EU and Eastern European countries – is one of the most ambitious that the EU has concluded with a third country. The agreement provides for the full liberalisation of 95 per cent of EU imports from South Africa by the end of a transitional period of 10 years, and for the full liberalisation of 96 per cent of South Africa's imports from the EU by the end of a transitional period of 12 years. While South Africa does not have access to EDF resources or to the Stabex and Sysmin funds, a total of 500 million euros were committed to the European Programme for Reconstruction and Development (EPRD) in South Africa for the period 1996 to 1999.

This agreement benefits South Africa in various ways. It will attract capital and technology. It will add credibility to its economy and economic policies. It provides South Africa with the benefits of membership to the Lomé Convention (such as participation in tenders for projects in all ACP countries and participation in all institutions of the Convention). The EU/South Africa free trade area (FTA) entails consistent trade reforms and could add credibility to the liberalisation programme. Furthermore, by eliminating the uncertainty factor for investors, the FTA might attract more capital.

In spite of these advantages, numerous problems remain. Agricultural products for which South Africa has a distinct comparative advantage are largely excluded from the agreement. Negotiations stumbled over 'sensitive' agricultural products from the EU standpoint (such as wine and spirits and fisheries), and over the duration of the transitional period for South Africa's full liberalisation (Gaudin 1997). Many manufactured goods already benefit from free access on the European market. This might result in a greater balance of trade deficit. Furthermore, the FTA might adversely affect the South African economy by leading to the elimination of uncompetitive industries, thereby increasing unemployment. Finally, the FTA must take into account the special relationship currently existing between South Africa and the other countries of southern Africa.

Ultimately, this agreement raises serious concerns for neighbouring southern African countries that are members of the Lomé Convention. The most immediate negative consequence would be a loss of customs revenues for the SACU member states through trade diversion and increased competition for exports and investment.

CONCLUSION: WHICH REGIONAL INTEGRATION AREA FOR SOUTH AFRICA?

There are currently three main regional centres of power in the world: the US in the Americas, the EU in Europe, and Japan and China in South East Asia. The question that arises is: with which of these centres should Africa entertain special relations? South Africa emerges as a secondary centre of power acting as interface between the African periphery and the three main centres. Should South Africa entertain privileged relationships with other southern African countries and take on the role of regional leader? Should it join Europe or, on the contrary, diversify its external relations and develop special relations with the emerging Asian economies?

Historically (through its Indian community), South Africa has always entertained close relations with Indian Ocean countries, as its membership of the Indian Ocean Rim (IOR, with Australia, India, Mauritius) clearly demonstrates. Fully 40 per cent of all direct foreign investment in South Africa comes from Asia. The IOR would thus have emerged as a credible alternative to special relations with the EU, had the negotiations with the latter failed.

Both South Africa and southern Africa have put in place many agreements and regional organisations which require further institutionalisation. Some of these organisations (such as the SACU and CMA) have a long history and are evolving in a radically changed environment. However, problems of dual membership and the incompatibility of different rules and regulations are emerging. The current liberalisation process is out of step with the many rules and policies of customs and monetary unions. Nevertheless, the main concerns are not of an institutional nature, but arise rather from South Africa's standing as a medium power and from the dynamism of a capitalism without equal in southern Africa. South Africa must also reconcile its role as regional leader with the urgent need to complete its own internal process of territorial, social and economic integration. The economic cost of affirmative action, the emerging African bourgeoisie, and unemployment reduction measures – over 40 per cent of secondary school-leavers are currently unemployed – entail significant financial costs which somewhat contradict South Africa's regional leadership role.

Africa is currently being marginalised, and short and medium-term interests are driving economic players towards the markets of industrialised or industrialising countries. However, in a context of deepening financial crisis and of the creation of regional blocs, privileged relationships with Africa are justified in terms of long-term geopolitical and economic interests. And while they might go against fashionable ideologies, the preservation of preferential relations should remain a priority.

In spite of an apparent protectionism, the African economies are effectively integrated into de facto free trade areas. National markets are open to contraband merchandise or low-priced goods. Given its current level of productivity and investment, Africa could not possibly sustain international competition without preferential agreements. It would thus seem that such agreements between Africa, the Caribbean and Pacific countries are fully justified and that, given the weight of the African states and of the EU, non-reciprocal agreements with Africa could be concluded within the WTO. Evidently, such reforms can only be meaningful if they lead to further European capital investment in Africa, and if Europe can have a growth contagion effect in Africa through the transfer of technology, and by opening up its markets to increasingly sophisticated African exports of manufactured goods.

---

1 Translation and updates by Guy Martin.
2 Editor's note: in view of the adoption, on 23 June 2000, of a new 20-year partnership agreement between the EU and the 77 ACP states (The Cotonou Agreement, see this whole section has been overtaken by events and, time and resources permitting, might need to be thoroughly updated. Note that having myself done much research on the Lomé Convention, I am quite familiar with the language used in the specialised literature on the subject, as a comparison of my translation with the original one will clearly indicate.
3 Editor's note: in March 1999, an EU/South Africa Trade, Development and Co-operation Agreement was concluded, the full text of which is available on the Internet. Note that I have revised the original French text accordingly.

Chapter Seven

BETWEEN CONFLICT AND CO-OPERATION: A STUDY OF FRANCO-SOUTH AFRICAN RELATIONS IN THE AFRICAN CONTEXT, 1990–1998

Chris Alden[1]

'I hope we shall be able to set in train what we have already called a partnership between South Africa and France.'
Francois Mitterrand, 4 July 1994.

'We are brothers.' Nelson Mandela, 4 July 1994.

The sea change in African politics since 1989, which has seen an array of authoritarian regimes give way to pluralist or populist governments with the active support of the international community, marks the effective end of the post-colonial period. In particular, the gradual unwinding of France's intimate relationship with its former colonies signals the diminution of direct extra-continental intervention in African affairs. At the same time, the emergence of South Africa as a continental power is a harbinger of new autarchy in the form and conduct of African politics with Pretoria serving as one of the centres of African power. Indeed, some would suggest that this decline in traditional French position and fortunes in Africa is directly linked to the rise in South African assertiveness on the continent and is in fact a prerequisite for South Africa to achieve its own continental ambitions.

This chapter will examine the changing nature of relations between France and South Africa regarding their respective Africa policies from 1990 to 1998. It will do so by examining the early period characterised by a promise of co-operation between the two powers; the emergence of conflicts of interest over Central Africa that have resulted in a dissolution of proposed co-operation; and an analysis of the future of the relationship.

THE PROMISE OF 'PARTNERSHIP', 1990–1994

As different as the two states are, France and South Africa nonetheless share some common features with regard to their respective place in the international system, especially so when it comes to their historical relationship with the African continent. France's 'African vocation' provided it with an ideological justification for its continuing and indeed intimate involvement in African affairs well after the twilight of official colonialism. Linked to this was a conscious effort to position France as an interlocutor between the industrialised North and the states of the Third World.[2] Like France, the South African government has at various times and under different regimes (colonial and apartheid) attempted to present itself as the gateway or European outpost on the continent, mediating between the interests of the West and those of Africa.[3]

Though obviously different in their relative capacities, as middle powers (on opposite ends of the capacity spectrum) both states have sought to utilise their relative economic, military and political power to shape events in Africa to their advantage. In the military sphere, the area where geo-strategists traditionally measure relative strength, France and South Africa have sought to develop their own arms manufacturing capacity, culminating in the creation of an independent nuclear capability, in order to be less unencumbered by external factors in pursuit of policy. In the economic sphere, both states have developed and supported 'captive' economies through the creation of subregional arrangements predicated upon currency linkages and providing for preferential concessions in terms of credit, tariff structures and market access. Finally, politically France and South Africa have, with varying degrees of success, attempted to give a broader political cast to their economic and military interests on the continent through the propagation of continental visions such as 'Euro-Afrique' and the 'African Charter'. In all these cases, the economic rationale often has been weaker than the drive to give expression to regional hegemonic interests over Africa.[4]

The historical particularities of Franco-South African relations are intimately bound up, on the one hand, with France's Africa policy and its own geo-strategic aims, and on the other hand, with South Africa's pursuit of apartheid on a continent shedding the shackles of colonialism. Under Charles de Gaulle and his immediate successors, a form of 'entente' was pursued with the National Party government in Pretoria that seemingly was in direct contradiction to France's established interests in francophone Africa. Co-operation ranged from diplomatic support at the OAU and UN to military assistance in the form of training programmes and the development of South Africa's indigenous weapons manufacturing capability, Armscor. Economic links involved not only substantial sales of military hardware but trade in technology as diverse as computers and nuclear energy, as well as agricultural and manufactured products. It was only with the collapse of Portuguese colonialism in 1974, and with it the failure of joint Franco-American-South African intervention to put into power a pro-Western government in Angola, that Paris began to reconsider its close ties with Pretoria.

Through the actions of the new Socialist government of Francois Mitterrand, French policy was to take a distinctive step away from Gaullist collaboration with Pretoria and open up a new relationship with both the African National Congress and the frontline states in 1981.[5] The expansion of the Franco-African summit process to include Luso and anglophone Africa, initiated under Giscard d'Estaing but embraced by Mitterrand, had the unexpected effect of introducing new pressures on France regarding its policy towards southern Africa. With the leaders of French-speaking Africa calling upon France to assume a more activist role in combating apartheid, Danielle Mitterrand sponsored a meeting of the African National Congress (ANC) and white South African dissidents in Dakar in 1987 aimed at paving the way for negotiations. The Franco-African summit held at La Baule in 1990 signalled a further commitment on the part of the French government to a new vision for its African partners that consciously sought to incorporate the emerging ethos of democratisation in its approach. This was followed by the deliberate de-linking of the French franc from the economies of former colonies in west-central Africa in 1994. At the same time, the incoming ANC government in South Africa indicated its strong support for the principles of democracy and human rights in the conduct of its foreign policy, while putting African interests at the forefront of its own positioning of South Africa in the international system.[6]

According to the French perspective, the convergence of interests over Africa argued for the development of a 'special relationship' between Paris and Pretoria in the post-Cold War era. The culmination of this extended courtship was the visit of Mitterrand to South Africa in 1994. As the first foreign head of state invited to post-apartheid South Africa and the first to address the new South African parliament, the French president was in a unique position to highlight the convergence of interests between the two powers over the continent of Africa. He took the opportunity to outline his vision of a Franco-South African entente:

> As you know, a conference will take place in Berlin on September 1994 ... bringing together the representatives of southern Africa, South Africa and the European Union so that, at last, we can give concrete effect to the interest we are taking in the renewal of your country. My ambition is that France should be at your side. There are, admittedly, many competing priorities, but this is an imperative because it is the fruit of intelligence and human courage. France offers to be your partner with her resources, but also with her ideals and that will, I hope, over the next century, enable us to strengthen the bonds we are building today. Within the international institutions, wherever peace and development are discussed and debated, we shall strive to be both your friends and your witnesses. As the French Republic we shall contribute to the best of our ability to the development of South Africa.[7]

And yet, within two years the evolving 'special relationship' between the two most powerful states operating in Africa had moved from the promise of 'partnership' towards open acrimony. In the wake of events in central Africa, South African officials consciously snubbed French initiatives in the Congo crisis, journalist accounts in South Africa lauded the demise of French influence in the continent, while privately South African diplomats voiced their satisfaction at the routing of 'French neocolonialism'.[8] This unanticipated development poses a number of questions:
- Why did the promise of co-operation dissolve into acrimony?
- Are French and South African interests, characterised by some as inherently contrary, in fact in conflict over their respective

policies towards Africa?
- What are the structural or institutional impediments to co-operation?

'PARTNERSHIP' POSTPONED: CONFLICT OVER CENTRAL AFRICA

The promise of Franco-South African co-operation proposed during the visit of Mitterrand in 1994, and bolstered by a wave of media speculation in France, failed to materialise. In part, this can be attributed to the visit itself which did not engendered the expected goodwill between the two states, but rather underscored the gap between French intentions and South African expectations. Indeed, it could be argued that the 'imperial style' adopted by the Mitterrand entourage during the visit, which clashed sharply with the populist approach of the new South African government in power, damaged the relationship from the outset.[9] However, while South African officials may have been disturbed by the conduct of some French officials and their French counterparts unhappy with the reception of their president, the actual undoing of relations was rooted in the two countries' conduct and ensuing dispute over the emerging crisis in Rwanda.

The complexities of the crisis in the Great Lakes region are better dealt with elsewhere.[10] Suffice it to say that French support for the Juvenal Habyarimana government against the Rwanda Patriotic Front incursions in the north of the country in 1993 translated, in the aftermath of Habyarimana's untimely death in April 1994, into assistance for the Hutu extremists (or *Interahamwe*) based in Rwanda and eastern Zaire. The documented evidence of French diplomatic, military and financial assistance to the perpetrators of mass killings of Tutsis and moderate Hutus in 1994 was followed by active support for Mobutu Sese Seko's attempts to hold onto power in Zaire in 1997. As the 37-year-old kleptocratic regime teetered towards collapse in the face of a combined Congolese, Rwandan and Ugandan force, French officials again inexplicably positioned themselves as opponents of populist change by supporting one of the most notorious dictators on the continent.

In more than one respect, the French approach to the crisis in the Great Lakes region of Central Africa was atavistic. Cast in terms of the 'Anglophone' threat to French interests in the region, the response to the Rwandan Patriotic Front's incursion into the tiny state was one which echoed all the worst features of French policy thought to have been expunged by the Socialist Party. The question as to why local French administrators were in a position in effect to act autonomously in the Rwandan crisis apparently has its roots in the bureaucratic politics of the Mitterrand administration. For historical reasons, France's Africa policy has been the product of several bureaucratic and political sources, among them the Ministry of Co-operation, the Ministry of Foreign Affairs and the Ministry of Defence. The absence of co-ordination between these bodies, notoriously evident in other African settings, reached tragic proportions in this case. At the same time, the culpability of the French government in support of a faction that promoted genocide is a fact that no amount of prevaricating can erase, as was made clear by a French parliamentary committee reviewing the French policy in Rwanda. As the Rwandan Minister of Defence, Paul Kagame, caustically but succinctly put it, 'If they (the French government) wanted people here to speak French, they shouldn't have helped to kill all those people here who spoke French.'[11]

With regard to the South African government, its approach to the crisis in the Great Lakes region reflected the state of institutional and political flux being experienced by the new democracy. With the traditional instruments of foreign policy, from the Department of Foreign Affairs, the Department of Trade and Industry and the Department of Defence all under review both in terms of policies and personnel, there was little scope for undertaking substantive action outside of South Africa's borders. The initial difficulty experienced by the African National Congress (ANC) in asserting control over policy making in a bureaucracy appointed during the apartheid era was compounded by its own lack of experience in exercising the reins of state power.[12] In specific terms, Nelson Mandela was approached by the American government at his inauguration in May 1994 to take action in Rwanda. Mandela demurred, saying that the utilisation of the SADF was impossible at that stage as it was still to undergo significant and far-reaching transformations. A year and a half later, the Canadian sponsored effort to muster together an international crisis intervention force in Burundi in 1996 received a more positive response from South Africa. While the Ministry of Defence claimed that it was unable to provide peacekeeping troops, it did allow for a token South African National Defence Force presence in the envisaged humanitarian intervention force.[13]

This being the said, it was clear to Pretoria that the ongoing nature of the crisis in the Great Lakes region warranted action of some kind if South Africa was to realise its ambitions to be a major player in continental affairs. Interestingly, and in contradiction to the officially stated policy regarding weapons sales, South African sources were active in providing armaments to the Rwandan military in advance of its combined incursion into Mobutu's Zaire in 1997.[14] This step was followed by an assertive role, backed by the United States (which also provided assistance to the anti-Mobutu forces), in facilitating negotiations between Laurent Kabila and Mobutu Sese Seko aimed at the peaceful transfer of power. The Outeniqua talks, which involved the South African president in a last minute bid to ensure that Kabila's Alliance des Forces Democratiques de Liberation du Congo-Zaire (AFDL) would not meet resistance from Mobutu's forces when it entered Kinshasa, demonstrated the growing self-confidence of South African diplomacy.

The post-Mobutu settlement, at least until Kabila's falling out with the government in Kigali, reflected the shifting balance of power between France and South Africa in the Zairean/Congolese and, more generally, continental affairs. One of Pretoria's first acts was to send a delegation of top government officials to Kinshasa both to assess the needs of Kabila's nascent regime and to offer assistance in rebuilding the country's shattered administrative and financial infrastructure. In 1998, the new Democratic Republic of the Congo joined the Southern African Development Community (SADC), an organisation increasingly oriented towards South Africa's dominant economy. With the Mobutu-era relations discredited, the new government in Kinshasa sought to cement commercial ties with new business partners from a host of sources, including South Africa, the United States and China, through the issuance of lucrative mineral concessions.[15] The severing of traditional links with French and Belgium companies, coupled with the ousting of civilian and military advisors to the government, were vivid symbols of the end of an era.

Thus the contrast was drawn between two responses to regional instability: France's recidivist approach towards the crisis, which focussed on shoring up the past through all means possible, and South Africa's approach, which backed 'populist' forces while employing mediation to achieve its ends. The hackneyed adage of 'African solutions to African problems', once consigned to the rhetoric of the independence period, seemed to be taking shape under a new leadership.[16] Significantly, South Africa's voice in the new configuration was one that emphasised democracy and human rights while employing conflict resolution and mediation. As Uganda's Yoweri Museveni famously declared at a gathering of leaders in Kinshasa, 'We are not francophone, we are not anglophone. We are bantuphone.'

THE FOREIGN POLICY OF CONTINENTAL AFFINITY: FROM EURO-AFRIQUE TO THE AFRICAN RENAISSANCE

While the proclaimed co-operative relationship proved stillborn in the face of circumstances, the governments in France and South Africa were themselves engaged in an extended review of their own foreign policy towards Africa. Despite a long-standing ambivalence towards the continent, both states have at various times in their respective histories used the concept of an 'African identity' to undergird their foreign policy in Africa. And yet, curiously, both states have managed to convey along with the utilisation of this label the fact of difference in distinguishing themselves from the rest of the continent. This foreign policy of affinity, declaiming a shared identity with Africa on the one hand and, concurrently, expressing a sense of 'otherness', is as much an ideology of domination as it is an expression of solidarity. Both states have traditionally 'engaged' Africa, that is they have couched their Africa policy in terms that intermingle identity and paternalism with the concept of regional hegemony. These continental visions, whether extra-regional as in the case of France as it reconfigured its colonial position in Africa, or South Africa, with its apartheid-era policies variously characterised as pursuing an African Charter, 'dialogue' or constructing a 'constellation of states', carry with them the seeds of continental ambitions.

In the case of France and the ideology of *'Euro-Afrique'*, the myths and institutions derivative of colonialism were found to be inadequate and the state is in the process (again) of reconsidering its Africa policy and its institutional manifestations. In fact, France's Africa policy had been under serious assault both from academic circles and sectors within the policy-making community since 1981. Arguably three events demonstrated the growing bankruptcy of France's *'Euro-Afrique'* approach. The first was the conscious de-linking of the economic arrangements that bound francophone Africa to the French currency and administrative apparatus in 1994. The second, the crisis in the Great Lakes, is discussed above. And finally, the third has been the response to the secessionist crisis in the Comoros Islands in mid-1997 and the Congo-Brazzaville. In the former case, France steadfastly ignored the pleas of the rebels on Anjou for formal re-incorporation into the French sphere of influence (something that would have drawn a positive response from the government in years past). In the case of the latter, it merely withdrew its own troops and citizens rather than actively support one faction as in the recent past, thus confirming its unwillingness to act unilaterally in continental affairs. Jacques Chirac sought to emphasise this fundamental change repeatedly in official declarations on the state's Africa policy from late 1996 onwards:

> It is no longer the role of any non-African country, whichever it is, to interfere. There must be a partnership ... (France and its former empire) have moved from an era of colonisation to an era of partnership and co-operation. That did not happen in a day but as a result of an evolution of events and of thinking ... In no case must the French army take sides in an internal political debate.[17]

This change, while perhaps still not fully reflected in the restructuring of the various institutions of French foreign policy making towards Africa, is nonetheless a significant sign that the ideology of *'Euro-Afrique'* is on the way to being buried. And with its demise comes the opportunity to put French relations with the continent on a new footing that will reflect current international realities and interests.

For South Africa, the end of apartheid and advent of a democratic government has meant that the myths and institutions that sustained its Africa policy must also be reshaped and dismantled. The belief that South Africa represented a European island in the midst of an African sea has given way to a new conception of South Africa's role on the continent. First voiced at the OAU summit in Tunis in 1994, the concept of an African renaissance received little attention until the collapse of Mobutu's regime in Zaire. Faced with impending change in Kinshasa, and under the influence of Museveni's visionary continental politics, the South African government began anew to address the matter of Africa's future. In so doing, the tentative utterings on the possibility of an African 'renewal' became the subject of public debate, receiving wide media coverage across South Africa. In a country hungry for hope, the prospect of a brighter political and economic future directed (at least in the early stages of discussion) implicitly by

South Africa, appealed to all sectors of the still fragmented society. Then Deputy-President Thabo Mbeki, heir apparent to the South African state, launched a dynamic programme both to publicise the concept and to flesh out some of its wider international, political and economic implications. Private seminars with leading figures in South Africa's foreign policy establishment were held and a pan-African conference, to include leaders from Museveni to Mugabe, was mooted. In the process, Mbeki imbued the concept with an imperative to continental activism on the part of South Africa.

> (T)he peoples of Africa entertain the legitimate expectation that the new South Africa, which they helped to bring into being, will not only be an expression of the African Renaissance by the manner in which it conducts its affairs, but will also be an active participant with other Africans in the struggle for the victory of that Renaissance throughout our continent.[18]

Although we are witnessing the demise of France's foreign policy of affinity, which was obviously more successful than apartheid South Africa's approach, it is worth analysing it as a guide to understanding the role of the ideology of affinity in the construction and implementation of foreign policy. In the first instance, the French experience highlights the dangers inherent in conceptualising one's Africa policy in terms of ideological imperatives. The seductive myths of France's 'African destiny' around which bureaucratic institutions and policies were promulgated from 1960 to the present served to obscure the actual nature of the forces driving the relationship. Lacking this critical awareness, French policy makers persisted in promoting an approach that was out of step with African realities while the French public struggled to interpret Franco-African relations through the imperfect lense of paternalism. Secondly, the French experience underscores the dangers inherent in basing one's foreign policy on personal relations. Close ties with Africa leaders afforded French presidents with a welcome assurance of support in the conduct of continental and international affairs, but it was a double-edged sword: French interests became tightly intertwined with those of their African allies and too often Paris found itself in the onerous position of defending a despot against his people. Finally, France's experience demonstrates the danger of allowing 'elite interests' alone to determine the conduct of foreign policy.

The misguided approaches adopted by Paris throughout the years as it sought to pursue (allegedly) national interest is a sobering reminder that the imperatives of bureaucracies and business – process, prestige and profit – are often the enemy of ' liberty, equality and fraternity'.

That having been said, the construction of new policies in Paris and Pretoria are, at best, still incomplete. In the case of France, there is solid evidence that the struggle to wrest policy from the control of the traditionalists appears to be being won by the reformists (see chapter by Guy Martin). In the case of South Africa, it would appear that the new government is intent on developing a foreign policy of affinity that takes account of the kind of concerns echoed above. In the words of the leading foreign policy think tank in South Africa:

> Foreign policy making under the democratically elected ANC government is dramatically different from the process under apartheid ... (T)he new South African government's foreign policy orientation after 1994 has been its commitment to become a true partner in southern Africa and support regional economic development processes.[19]

By adopting an approach to continental foreign policy that forswears the shibboleths of the past, France and South Africa are laying the foundation for a constructive relationship based on African realities. Dispensing with residual colonial myths and purging the notion of affinity of its paternalistic dimensions allows the possibility for the two states to engage Africa on terms that foster genuine partnership in pursuit of their respective Africa policies.

FORGING NEW RELATIONS

In the aftermath of the crisis in central Africa, frosty relations between Paris and Pretoria have been slow to warm. In the first instance, concrete steps have been taken to put the relationship on a political footing with the establishment of the Forum on Political Dialogue in October 1997. Despite this accomplishment, there was some disquiet among French circles at the fact that the South African government did not agree to create a bi-national commission, as was the case with the United States and other key countries such as India.[20] South Africa's active role in the Franco-African summit process is a further signal of its willingness to participate in one of Africa's leading political forums, and one which is especially close to the French foreign policy community. The continuing importance France places on maintaining a presence in the Indian Ocean (where it retains sovereign control over some of the islands) has argued for its active inclusion in the developing regional arrangements known as the Indian Ocean Rim Initiative.

Commercial ties between the two countries continue to increase, with over 400 new French companies establishing themselves in South Africa since the ending of apartheid. Overall Franco-South African trade is growing with French imports to South Africa doubling from R3 890 000 in 1996 to R6 310 000 in 1998 and South African exports to France shooting up from R1 640 000 in 1996 to R2 870 000 in 1998[21]. Furthermore, with South Africa identified by the French Development Agency as one of its seven priority emerging market countries, French investments have made it the seventh largest investor in South Africa. Notably, the rate of French investment in South Africa, now the largest African destination for French capital, is in marked contrast to the steady withdrawal of French interests in the *'pre-carre'*.[22] The resentment initially felt by South African officials over France's role in blocking the trade agreement with the European Union in the contentious area of agricultural products has dissipated with the signing of the accord in 1999. This has, however, to some extent been replaced, according to South African analysts, by a 'rivalry...on the African continent between South African and French businessmen'.[23]

In the area of security, the failure to win the contract to re-equip the new South African National Defence Force dealt a blow to the hopes of the French armaments industry. At the same time, South African participation in the RECAMP (Reinforcement du Capacite d'Armees Africaines de Maintenir la Paix) exercise, the French Ministry of Defence's peacekeeping training programme, marks the onset of a co-operative relationship in the area of security. Despite this, the South African National Defence Force remains fundamentally oriented towards the British.

The clash of French and South African interests recently experienced in central Africa only underscores the death of an old order without the concomitant complete emergence of a new one in its stead. As a measure of the tyranny of the past over contemporary policy, France's tarnished relations with the continent are only now emerging from an unprecedented level of disarray. The question may nonetheless be asked as to whether France will continue to maintain its traditional interest in continental affairs. If it is to do so, then it must obviously be on a different basis from the past and must exhibit a clear break with that past.

At the same time, South Africa's own capacity to articulate its interests with regard to Africa and, beyond that, implement coherent polices on that basis remain at a point of gestation.[24] South African analysts, perhaps exhibiting the hubris too often associated with a newly democratic country, have suggested that:

> Regardless of the inevitable suspicions and intrigues that pervade African politics, South Africa's profile as a regional superpower and the economic powerhouse of Africa amply equips it with the ability to forge relationships with virtually all African countries alike. In a very real sense, France needs South Africa more than South African needs France when it comes to the consolidation and extension of francophone influence in Africa.[25]

Indeed, it is possible that the road to France's rehabilitation with those African political circles that are intent on shaping the future destiny of the continent lies through Pretoria. More likely, however, is that the new Anglo-Franco initiative on Africa, announced in St Malo and followed by a joint visit to the continent by the British and French foreign ministers in March 1999, including the co-ordination of policy and sharing of embassy facilities, is Paris's preferred route.[26]

For all the hackneyed and shopworn quality of the Gaullist idea of 'trilangularism', there exists a basis for deeper co-operation between Paris and Pretoria in continental matters. Whether this will translate into active policy co-ordination of the kind broached by hopeful French officials in 1994 remains to be seen. However, with growing co-ordination between the British and French foreign ministries in the conduct and formulation of their Africa policies, the cost of South Africa remaining aloof from Europe and, concurrently, Europe turning its back on South Africa is too high to be counted.

---

1. The author would like to thank *the Institut francais de l'Afrique du Sud* (Johannesburg) and the *Departemente scientifiques sociales, Ecole Normale Superieure* (Cachan) for generously sponsoring research on this topic.
2. For a detailed description of the evolution of French policy towards the South, see Jacques Adda and Marie-Claude Smouts, *La France face au Sud: Le miroir brise* Paris: Karthala 1989, pp 109–145.
3. James Barber and John Barratt, *South Africa's Foreign Policy: the Search for Status and Security, 1945–1988* Cambridge: Cambridge UP 1990, pp 18–19; 34–44.

4   Serge Michailof, ed., *La France et l'Afrique: vade-mecum pour un nouveau voyage* (Paris: Karthala 1993).
5   See Chris Alden, 'From Policy Autonomy to Policy Integration' in Chris Alden and Jean-Pascal Daloz, eds., *Paris, Pretoria and the African Continent: the International Relations of States and Societies in Transition* (Basingstoke: Macmillan 1996).
6   See African National Congress, 'Foreign Policy in a New South Africa: a Discussion Paper', Department of International Affairs, ANC, October 1993; Nelson Mandela, 'South Africa's Future Foreign Policy', *Foreign Affairs*, November/December 1993.
7   Speech by Francois Mitterrand to parliament of South Africa, 4 July 1994, photocopy.
8   *Weekly Mail and Guardian* 29 January 1997; *Weekly Mail and Guardian*, 13 December 1996; various interviews with South African officials.
9   Interview with senior South African diplomat, Paris, 27 October 1998.
10 See, for example, Claude Kabemba, 'Whither the DRC? Causes of Conflict in the Democratic Republic of the Congo, and the Way Forward', *Policy: Issues and Actors*, 12:1, Centre for Policy Studies, Johannesburg, March 1999.
11 Cited in Philip Gourevitch, 'Letter from the Congo: Continental Shift', *The New Yorker*, 4 August 1997, p. 48.
12 Paul-Henri Bischoff and Roger Southall, 'The Early Foreign Policy of the Democratic South Africa' in Stephen Wright, ed., *African Foreign Policies* Boulder, CO: Westview 1999, pp 156–159.
13 Interview with senior member of Intelligence Directorate, Ministry of Defence, Pretoria, 10 May 1997.
14 *The Star*, 16 April 1998.
15 *Weekly Mail and Guardian* 15 April 1997; *The Star* (Johannesburg) 25 July 1997.
16 Marina Ottaway, *Africa's New Leaders: Democracy or State Reconstruction?* Washington, D.C.: Carnegie Endowment for International Peace, 1999, pp 109–116.
17 Jacque Chirac at the Franco-African summit, Ouagadougou, Niger, as reported in *Agence France-Presse*, 7 December 1996.
18 Speech by the Deputy-President of South Africa, Thabo Mbeki, 'The African Renaissance: South Africa and the World', United Nations University, 9 April 1998, p. 16.
19 Garth le Pere, Kato Lambrechts and Anthoni van Nieuwkerk, 'South Africa's Foreign Policy Challenges in the New Millennium', *Global Dialogue* 4:3 December 1999, pp 3–4.
20 Interview with senior South African diplomat, Paris, October 1997.
21 *South African Yearbook of International Affairs, 1999/2000* Braamfontein: South African Institute of International Affairs 1999, p. 447.
22 *The Star* (Johannesburg) 26 June 1998.
23 *The Sunday Independent* (Johannesburg) 10 May 1998.
24 Le Pere et al, op. cit., 7–8.
25 Rockyn Williams, 'From Huguenots to Humanism: Franco-South Africa Security Dialogue' *South African Journal of International Affairs* 6:2 Winter 1999, p. 122.
26 *Financial Times* 12 March 1999.

PART THREE:
FRANCE AND SOUTH AFRICA: ISSUES AND CHALLENGES

Chapter Eight

THE LANGUAGE OF 'FRANCOPHONIE' AND THE RACE OF THE RENAISSANCE: A COMMONWEALTH PERSPECTIVE

Ali A. Mazrui

What was unique about *francophonie* until the 1990s was that it was the only international and intergovernmental club based on **linguistic apartheid**. In concept, *'francophonie'* was based on a vision that the world consisted of two kinds of nations – French-speaking and the other aliens. No other community of nations was conceived in such stark linguistic terms. On the other hand, South Africa until the 1990s was a country based on **racial apartheid**. The underlying vision was that humanity consisted of a hierarchy of races with whites at the top, blacks at the very bottom, and other races such as Indians and those of mixed ethnicity in-between. From 1948 onwards no other country in the world conceived of itself in such stark racially segregationist terms.

What has happened with *'francophonie'* in the 1990s is that linguistic criteria of admission to the club have been considerably loosened. Indeed the principle of linguistic apartheid may have been abandoned altogether. However, in South Africa there has been the demise of the political aspects of racial apartheid, but the economic aspects of apartheid have remained resilient.

The central politics of *francophonie* has been the politics of language. The central politics of the African renaissance has been the politics of race. The Commonwealth has been caught up in the politics of race and civil liberties.

FRANCOPHONIE AND THE COMMONWEALTH

If *francophonie* promoted linguistic apartheid based on the French language, why did the Commonwealth not promote/encourage a similar apartheid system based on the English language? Although English is indeed the official language of the Commonwealth (it is also one of the six official languages of the United Nations), the main qualification for Commonwealth membership was until the 1990s historic rather than linguistic. Members of the Commonwealth had to have directly shared the experience of British imperial history (Britain as the former imperial power and the other as former colonies). No linguistic credentials were needed, either *de jure* or de facto. Indeed, when India became a member in 1947, Hindi was intended to replace English in India in stages. When Tanganyika (now Tanzania) became independent in 1961, Julius K Nyerere was committed to increasing Swahilization. And when Cyprus became independent in 1961, Greek and Turkish languages did replace English as the official languages.

In its earlier phases *francophonie* also seemed to be based on qualifications of shared history, but the shared language was always important for France. The earlier membership consisted almost entirely of France and its former empire, but linguistic solidarity mattered. As membership expanded, the qualifications of shared language superseded the qualifications of shared imperial history. In Africa, the former Belgian dependencies of Congo (Kinshasa), Rwanda and Burundi were next for incorporation into the fraternity of *francophonie*. The official language of the former Belgian colonies was of course French.

The Commonwealth was born long before most of Africa became independent. Ironically, the first full African member of the Commonwealth was South Africa under white rule, going back to Commonwealth origins under the Statute of Westminster enacted by the British parliament in 1931. White-ruled Southern Rhodesia (now Zimbabwe) subsequently became an associate member of the Commonwealth long before Ghana was admitted as the first black-led member in 1957.

A minimum of democratic culture was one of the qualifications for continuing membership of the Commonwealth – as distinct from a minimum of the French language as a credential for continuing association with *francophonie*. From 1936 to 1961 the minimum of democratic culture in the Commonwealth was sometimes limited to the white electorate of a particular member country. This was certainly true of the Union of South Africa and, in a different sense, of Australia at one true. It was also true of the white electorate of the associate member of Southern Rhodesia. Parliamentary democracy was practised, but within racial limits. In 1947, India and Pakistan provided the first non-white governments admitted to membership of the Commonwealth, and in 1957 Ghana became the first black government. But South Africa was still a member, with parliamentary democracy still confined mainly to the white electorate. It was not until 1961, when South Africa was forced to withdraw from the Commonwealth, that respect for racial equality became a qualification for remaining in the Commonwealth. Ironically parliamentary democracy was already under severe stress in the new non-white Commonwealth. In Pakistan the military was already exercising disproportionate power. And in Ghana and Tanzania theories were soon to emerge justifying single-party democracies.

1961 brought commitment to racial equality as a qualification for membership of the Commonwealth. For a while this new principle seemed to overshadow the older principle of commitment to democracy. Before long the Commonwealth's most passionate foreign policy crusade became the struggle against apartheid in South Africa. Summit meeting after summit meeting of the Commonwealth was dominated by the issue of apartheid. During the years of Margaret Thatcher there was a persistent cleavage between her government (reluctant to impose sanctions on South Africa) and much of the rest of the Commonwealth. There was a time when South Africa seemed destined to experience one of the bloodiest examples of *primary* civil wars – an actual racial war appeared inevitable. After all, everywhere else in Africa where there had been a large white minority there had been severe bloodshed before full majority rule was realised. Kenya experienced the Mau Mau war (1952–1960); Algeria experienced its war of independence (1954–1962); Rhodesia and Angola had their equivalent conflicts. Since South Africa had the largest white minority of all, how could it possibly avert the same bloodstained fate?

However, one particular difference turned out to be more relevant than many people imagined. The whites of South Africa identified themselves with Africa, but not with the Africans. The

Afrikaners especially were passionately loyal to the African soil (the land), but not to the African blood (the indigenous people). In contrast, the whites of colonial Algeria were nascent *'francophonie'*. They were loyal neither to Africa nor to the Africans. Their loyalty was to France. They owed no special allegiance to the soil of Africa except as a means of livelihood. They certainly owed no loyalty to the blood of the indigenous peoples. They attempted to turn Africa into an extension of France. Was this *francophonie* become anti-African?

Similarly the whites of Angola attempted to turn their part of Africa into an extension of Portugal. This is in contrast to those whites of South Africa who identified themselves with the African soil so much that they called themselves Afrikaners, and even attempted to monopolise the name 'Africans' for themselves. Actually anglophone whites were only marginally better than francophone whites in their loyalty to Africa. White Rhodesians were simply too British, many of them enjoying dual citizenship for the duration of Ian Smith's Unilateral Declaration of Independence (UDI). Of all the whites of Africa perhaps only the Afrikaners had evolved a relationship with the African land. The Afrikaners mixed their sweat mystically with the African soil, but did not mix their blood spiritually with that of the African people.

How did South Africa then avert a racial war in the twentieth century? One reason was indeed cultural. It was the simple fact that the Afrikaners were halfway towards Africanisation through a marriage between the Afrikaner **soul** and the African **soil** . They avoided the white colonial Algerian sin of identifying both the **soul** and the **Algerian soil** with France.

A second reason why South Africa averted a racial war in the twentieth century is essentially a division of labour between black political power and white economic privilege. The white man said to the black man: 'You take the crown, and I will keep the jewels.' The black man was to acquire the political crown, while the white man retained the economic jewels. In many ways, while political apartheid has ended, economic apartheid is still intact. The best land, the best mines, the best jobs, the best shops and commercial opportunities are still overwhelmingly in white hands or under white control. The challenge for the post-Mandela South Africa is how to dismantle economic apartheid without causing widespread economic and social havoc. Perhaps this is the supreme challenge of the African renaissance in southern Africa.

While most people are convinced that South Africa indeed averted a primary civil war (white versus blacks) in the twentieth century, can one be complacent about averting it in the twenty-first century if economic apartheid remains intact? The twenty-first century may not have the moral leadership of the rank of Nelson Mandela. However, it may still have the valuable resource of the marriage between the Afrikaner soul and the African soil.

This brings us to the third reason why South Africa averted a racial war in the twentieth century and concerns Africa's short memory of hate. Cultures vary considerably in their ability to retain hate. The Irish have a long retention of memories of atrocities perpetrated by the English. The Armenians have longstanding memories about atrocities committed against them by the Turks in the Ottoman Empire. The Jews have extensive memories about their martyrdom in history. On the other hand, Jomo Kenyatta proceeded to forgive his British tormentors very quickly after being released from unjust imprisonment. He even published a book entitled *Suffering without bitterness*. Where but in Africa could somebody like Ian Smith, who had unleashed a war which killed many thousands of black people, remain free after the attainment of black majority rule to torment his black successors whose policies had killed far fewer people than his politicies had done?

Is a short memory of hate a precondition for the African renaissance? Nelson Mandela lost 27 of the best years of his life. Yet on being released he was not only in favour of reconciliation between blacks and whites, but he went to beg the white terrorists who were fasting to death not to do so; and he went out of his way to pay his respects to Mrs Verwoerd, the widow of the architect of apartheid. Is Africa's short memory of hate sometimes too short? Is it nevertheless necessary for the African renaissance? What really saved South Africa from a primary racial war in the twentieth century? It was mainly a convergence of those three forces – the mystical relationship between the Afrikaner soul and the African soil; the black African's short memory of hate, and the historic bargain which conceded the political crown to the blacks and kept the economic jewels with the whites at least for this century.

Was there a fourth reason why South Africa avoided a racial war? Was the fourth reason the international sanctions against South Africa? In this case it was not the **soul** of the Commonwealth, but its **conscience** which served as the vanguard of international action against apartheid in South Africa.

FROM 'EURAFRICA' TO FRANCOPHONIE

France invented the concept of 'Eurafrica' – asserting an organic relationship between Europe and Africa, deep enough to transform the two continents into a single integrated international subsystem. How does this concept relate to the French language? How does this concept relate to *francophonie*.

'Eurafrica' became the core of *francophonie*. The majority of French-speaking people in the world are in the western world – mainly in France itself. However, the majority of French-speaking **states** are in Africa. Over 20 members of the Organization of African Unity are French-speaking in the sense of having adopted French as an official language. These are Algeria, Benin, Burundi, Chad, Cameroon, Central African Republic, Comoros, Congo, Coté d'Ivoire, Djibouti, Burkina Faso, Gabon, Guinea, Malagasy, Mali, Mauritania, Morocco, Niger, Rwanda, Senegal, Réunion, Togo, Tunisia and the Democratic Republic of Congo (formerly Zaire). Without Africa the French language would be almost a provincial language. The Democratic Republic of Congo (DRC) is the largest French-speaking country after France in population – and destined to be the largest by all accounts early in the twenty-first century. If the Congo succeeds in stabilising itself, and in assuming effective control over its resources, it may become France's rival in influence and power in French-speaking Africa as a whole. Indeed, the DRC (Kinshasa) could become a major force in *francophonie* as a whole. When one looks at this global scene, the French language is declining in influence as a language. On the other hand, *francophonie* as a fraternity of states is expanding in membership and purpose. Let us take each of these propositions in turn: firstly, why French is declining in Europe and the North as a whole; and secondly, why *franocphonie* as a 'club' is expanding?

The most important challenge to the French language in the northern hemisphere has been caused by the tremendous increase in American influence in the twentieth century. The American language has of course been English. While the spread of the English language in Africa was mainly due to the impact of imperial Britain, the spread of the English language in East and South East Asia and in Europe, and its increasing role in international affairs, has been largely due to the new American hegemony in the world. The triumph of the English language globally has ranged from increasing usage in diplomacy to its pre-eminent role as the supreme language of aviation and air control.

A related reason for the shrinkage of French in world affairs concerns the computer revolution and the Internet. The amount of information circulating in English is so much greater than what is transmitted in French that English is gaining even greater ascendancy. The old adage that 'nothing succeeds like success' has now been computerised. The global influence of American computer firms like IBM and Microsoft has reinforced this anglo-computer revolution.

At the other end of social concerns is the decline of the cultural influence of the upper classes in Europe. Royal houses in continental Europe as a whole had once preferred to use the French language extensively. In the aftermath of the Russian Revolution in 1917 and the subsequent development of social egalitarianism in Europe as a whole, linguistic snobbery declined, and pragmatism became the norm. Aristocratic snobbery had once favoured French; egalitarian linguistic pragmatism in continental Europe was later to favour the English language.

The fourth factor behind the decline of French especially in the northern hemisphere has been Britain's entry into the European Economic Community (later European Union). This has made English more decisively one of the official languages of the community. The new language, both written and oral, became increasingly influential in the affairs of the European Union. Smaller members of the union have more frequently turned to English rather than French in the post-Gaullist era of European affairs.

The fifth factor behind the decline of French in the northern hemisphere is linked to the decline of the power of the French-speaking Walloons in Belgium. The days of French pre-eminence in Belgium were coming to an end in the 1980s, although francophone Brussels still remained the capital of the country. Belgium moved towards a neo-federal structure, rooted in the principle of linguistic parity between French and Flemish. It is arguable that in North America the French language has made some gains as a result of the greater recognition of bilingualism in the whole federation of Canada. On the other hand, there has been a decline of linguistic nationalism in Quebec since the old militancy of the 1960s. And the French of Quebec has become increasingly contaminated by Anglicisms. The Quebec language is genuinely under siege.

The decline of the role of German in Europe has also tended to favour English rather than French. When the Scandinavian countries regarded German virtually as their first foreign language, there was a tendency to invest in the French language as well for a sense of balance. But when the Scandinavians turned more decisively to the English language as their first foreign tongue, it was not just German which suffered; it was also French. Since English was in any case more widely used than German, its adoption by the Scandinavians as the premier foreign language reduced the need to 'balance' it with French.

Of course, the Scandinavians are greater linguists than the average in any case. Their schools are still sensitised to the importance of French and German as well as English. But linguistic priorities have indeed changed in the Nordic syllabuses and curricula – and in class enrolments. The English language has definitely been the main beneficiary of the decline of German – and the French language has also sustained a decline in educational emphasis.

Japan too has experienced shifts in emphasis that have demoted German and French – and raised the role of English in educational and linguistic priorities. Between the Meiji Restoration in 1868 and Japan's defeat in World War II in 1945, Japan's main western role models were indeed Germany and France. This Franco-German orientation affected not only Japan's curricula and syllabi, but also profoundly influenced its legal system and civil code. It was the American occupation of Japan (1945–1952) which decisively shifted Japan from a Franco-German role model to the Anglo-Saxon alternative. The United States's continuing special relationship with Japan after the post-war occupation consolidated Japan's cultural reorientation. While the Americans under Douglas MacArthur imposed upon Japan in 1947 a national constitution basically drawn from continental European experience, much of the rest of the westernisation of Japan has been a case of cultural Americanisation – from the introduction of baseball to the Japanese enthusiasm for American pop stars. The very economy of Japan has interlocked itself with the American economy. The confirmation of the English language as Japan's first western language in the post-war era has been part of this American phase of Japan's transformation. The decline of the French and German languages in Japanese priorities was an inevitable consequence of the Americanisation of Japan. A particularly surprising development was the decision of the Socialist Party of Japan to adopt a campaign anthem written in the English language in the election campaign for the Lower House in 1989–1990. It marked the beginning of a new role for English in Japanese politics.

In the Great Lakes area of Africa the French language also sustained setbacks in the 1990s. Political leadership in Rwanda was captured by anglophone Tutsi who had grown up and been educated in Uganda. English had a new political role in Rwanda. So did Kiswahili in the post-Mobutu Congo.

If these have been the main factors which have resulted in the decline of the French language in the northern hemisphere, which factors have contributed to the simultaneous expansion and consolidation of *francophonie*? What indeed is *francophonie*?

Twenty-one French-speaking countries coalesced as an intergovernmental organisation for co-operation and created *francophonie* in March 1970. The initial official name of the organisation was *l'Agence de Cooperation Culturelle et Technique (ACCT)* [Agency for Cultural and Technical Co-operation]. Current membership includes 49 member countries and three countries with observer status – Albania, Macedonia and Poland. Major institutional reforms were decided upon during the Hanoi summit (14–16 November 1997). Following these reforms, ACCT became *l'Agence de la Francophonie* (Agency of the *Francophonie*). The old purely administrative secretariat general under the ACCT was elevated to a more visible and political status, and it is now called the *Secretariat General de la Francophonie* (General Secretariat of the *Francophonie*) reporting directly to the conference of heads of states and governments, and the ministerial conference.

The *Agence de la Francophonie* is headed by an *Administrateur Général* (General Administrator) appointed by the General Conference for four years, and the appointment is renewable. The administrator runs the programmes and day-to-day operations of the agency. The first appointed general administrator under the new formula is Roger Dehaybe, from Belgium. The *Secrétariat Général de la Francophonie* has as head a secretary general who is the political spokesperson and official representative of the *francophonie* at the international level. Former United Nations Secretary General Boutros Boutros Ghali, an Egyptian, was elected at the Hanoi summit as the first secretary general of the *francophonie*. There is no official indication that the general administrator must come from the North and the secretary general from the South, but non-official sources, such as the media, have suggested that sort of division of labour.

What must be emphasised in the first instance is that the southern expansion of *francophonie* is particularly strong in Africa. On the whole the distribution of the French language is bi-continental – there are large number of French-speaking individuals in

Europe, and large number of French-speaking states in Africa. Europe and Africa are by far the primary constituencies of *francophonie*. Of course there are smaller francophone constituencies in Quebec, Lebanon, Syria, Indochina and elsewhere, but these are the peripheries of the francophone world. The main theatre of action is Europe and Africa.

The historical factors which have favoured expansion in Africa have included the type of states which French and Belgian imperialism created during the colonial period. These were often multi-ethnic countries which needed a lingua franca. Colonial policy had chosen the French language as the lingua franca – and the entire educational system and domestic political process consolidated that linguistic choice. A related factor was the assimilationist policy of France as an imperial power. This created an elite mesmerised by French culture and civilisation. A surprising number still retained dual citizenship with France even after independence. If President Bokassa was anything to go by, some African heads of state may secretly still be citizens of France. As an aspect of the cultural lifestyle of the *francophonie*, annual holidays in France continue to be part of the elite culture of francophone West and North Africa.

With some subsidies and technical assistance, the French language is also featuring more and more in classrooms in Commonwealth Africa. Before independence British educational policy makers were more committed to the promotion of indigenous African languages than to the promotion of the rival French legacy in British colonies. Nor were French offers of language teachers for schools in British colonies welcomed. The global French fraternity of *francophonie* now has, as we indicated, a secretariat in Paris partly headed by an African, Boutros Boutros Ghali. There is a parallel administrative agency headed by somebody else. Membership of the *francophonie* club now includes countries which have not adopted French as a national language, but which can be persuaded to teach more French in their schools.

The difference which Africa's independence has made is partly in a greater readiness on the part of anglophone governments to accept France's offers of teachers of the French language. Many an African university in the Commonwealth has been the beneficiary of technical assistance and cultural subsidies from the local French embassy or directly from France. Portuguese-speaking Africa is even more responsive to the attractions of *francophonie*.

France's policy in Africa is consolidated partly through an aggressive cultural diplomacy. Considerable amounts of money are spent on French-style syllabi and curricula in African schools, and on the provision of French teachers, advisers and reading materials. A residual French economic and administrative presence in most former French colonies has deepened Africa's orientation towards Paris. In addition, every French president since Charles de Gaulle has attempted to cultivate special personal relations with at least some of the African leaders. There is little doubt that French-speaking African presidents have greater and more personalised access to the French president than their anglophone counterparts have had to either the British prime minister or the British head of state, the Queen, in spite of Commonwealth conferences. Here again is a case of reciprocal conquest. In spite of the global decline of French, there is little doubt that the French language and culture have conquered large parts of Africa. Many decisions about the future of Africa are being made by people deeply imbued with French values and perspectives.

Indeed, *francophonie* is expanding its constituency in Africa, at least outside Algeria. It is true that the post-colonial policy of re-Arabisation in Algeria is designed to increase the role of Arabic in schools and public affairs at the expense of the pre-eminent colonial role of the French language. The rise of Islamic militancy in Algeria may pose new problems to aspects of French culture. It is also true that the late Mobutu Sese Seko's policy of promoting regional languages in the old Zaire (Lingala, Kikongo, Tshiluba and Kiswahili) was partly at the expense of French in Zairean (now Congolese) curricula. We also mentioned how from 1994 French has suffered a setback in Rwanda, led by anglophone Tutsi originally educated in Uganda. But such setbacks for French in Africa are compatible with the expansion of *francophonie* as a 'club' of states. On the whole French is still a major presence in Africa, though the pace of its expansion has drastically declined.

However, when all is said and done, France's aspiration to remain a global power requires a cultural constituency as well as an economic one. It seems likely that the 1990s will continue to signify a change in France's economic priorities in favour of the new pan-European opportunities and against the older investments in Africa. It seems equally certain that a more open Europe after the end of the Cold War will favour the English language at the expense of the French language even within France itself. As the custodian of the fortunes of French civilisation, France could not afford to abandon the cultural constituency of *francophonie* entirely in favour of the more open Europe. The collapse of the Soviet Empire has been a further gain for the English language. France may need Africa more culturally, but less economically.

With its cultural constituency in Europe declining, its cultural constituency in Africa has become more valuable than ever as the centrepiece of *francophonie*. A remarkable interdependence has emerged – still imperfect and uneven, but real enough to make Africa indispensable for the recognition of France as a truly global power and the acceptance of the French language as a credible world language. 'Eurafrica' as a concept gets part of its meaningfulness from the destiny of *francophonie*. As a language French may be in decline; but as an international cultural club *francophonie* is expanding and becoming more institutionalised.

From the point of view of *francophonie* and the Commonwealth, Egypt has been almost unique. This is a country which was only briefly occupied by the French following Napoleon's invasion of 1798. On the other hand, Egypt was occupied by Great Britain for a much longer period, beginning in 1882 until formal independence in 1923, and then partially controlled by Britain in one way or another until the Egyptian Revolution of 1952. And yet Egypt today is a member of the *francophonie* (in spite of the brevity of French rule) and not a member of the Commonwealth (in spite of more than half a century of British control). In a sense it is easier to see why no Arab country previously ruled by Britain chose to join the Commonwealth than to explain why Egypt subsequently chose to join the *francophonie*. Most Arab leaders regarded the Commonwealth as a continuation of the British Empire, and therefore the face of neocolonialism. Many Arabs also blamed the British (the mandated power in Palestine) for not trying harder to prevent the partition of Palestine and the creation of the state of Israel. And when Egypt was under a revolutionary Nasserite regime from 1952 to 1970, it was more unlikely than ever that Egypt would want to have anything to do with the Commonwealth.

Under Gamal Abdel Nasser, Egypt did not want to be much associated with France either – not in the wake of the Suez invasion of 1956 and the Algerian war of independence of 1954–1962. However, among the wider social elite of Egypt there was always a fascination with France – what might be called the Napoleon-De Lesseps-Aida complex. De Lesseps was the French engineer who designed the Suez Canal. It was opened in 1869 by the Empress Eugénie, consort of Napoleon III. The Khedive of Egypt, to celebrate the opening of the canal, commissioned Giusseppe Verdi to compose an opera. The masterpiece was *Aida*, produced in Cairo in 1871, a glittering French-Italian-Ottoman occasion. Although *Aida* as an opera was Italian, its link with the opening of the Suez Canal gallicised it in the Egyptian imagination. It was this triple complex – the mystique of Napoleon's brief occupation of Egypt, the French role in the building of the Suez Canal, and the superb opera which was created to celebrate the opening of the canal – which contributed to keeping alive among some sectors of the Egyptian elite an enduring fascination with France. Schools based on the French language have continued to the present day; so have aspects of the Napoleonic code in the Egyptian legal system. All this goes part of the way towards explaining why Egypt in the last quarter of the twentieth century was at last ready to join the *francophonie* – although Egypt has never seriously considered joining the Commonwealth.

THE ORIGINS OF THE AFRICAN RENAISSANCE

When did the African renaissance begin? One important date is Africa's recapture of the Suez Canal in 1956. Gamal Abdel Nasser nationalised the waterway which had been built not just by a French engineer called De Lesseps, but also by hundreds of Egyptian workers, many of whom lost their lives.

In francophone Africa the genesis of the African renaissance was courageous in a different way. It was the vote for independence by the people of Guinea (Conakry) in 1958, thereby defying the massive French pressure to vote the other way. The people of Guinea stood alone in their preference for sovereignty, although their leader Sékou Touré later let them down by becoming a tyrant.

For Commonwealth Africa the African renaissance began when Nigeria demonstrated that Africa could be plunged into a civil war and have a one-man 'Truth and Reconciliation Commission' – Yakubu Gowon. Although Gowon presided over the Nigerian civil war, he was more than Africa's Abraham Lincoln. During the conflict he was constantly worried about civilian casualties on both sides, though modern war has that propensity. He constantly discouraged the federal propaganda machine from describing the Biafrans as the enemy. And when the war ended he insisted that there were to be no reprisals, no Nuremberg trials, no victimisation of the vanquished. By an ironic twist of fate, after the war General Gowon became a hero to many Igbos, the former Biafran secessionists.

If there is an African renaissance we should also be impressed by what Gowon did when he was overthrown in a military coup in 1975. Former heads of state who have the humility to go back to school should be part of the African renaissance. Gowon went to become a university undergraduate. The same man who had been honoured by Cambridge University in England with an honorary doctorate as a head of state was standing in a cafeteria line at Warwick University a few years later as an undergraduate. I first met him in his undergraduate but post-presidential days. He continued his studies at Warwick right up to his PhD. Gowon had qualities worthy of the African Renaissance. He was truly a one-man 'Truth and Reconciliation Commission'.

And if General Dr Gowon had seen something in others worth saluting, it was mainly because there was so much greatness in Gowon himself. As the poet said:

> When the high heart we magnify
> And the sure vision celebrate
> And worship greatness passing by
> Ourselves are great

The only Nigerian head of state who first came to power as a military ruler and was later freely elected is another soldier, General Olusegun Obasanjo. Is the transition from military ruler to a freely elected civilian ruler a kind of renaissance? That is arguable. But Obasanjo's earlier moral claims were more compelling. They were established in 1979. It may be asked what the African renaissance has to learn from General Obasanjo himself. The answer is that he gave up political power voluntarily. This was exactly 20 years before Nelson Mandela did the same thing.

General Obasanjo was not only the first African military ruler voluntarily to organise elections and hand over to a civilian administration, but he was the first African head of state of any kind to voluntarily relinquish power, and, at that, to somebody not of his own choosing. Both Leopold Senghor of Senegal and Julius K Nyerere of Tanzania were subsequently to hand over power to people who had needed their prior approval as heirs. But in Nigeria it has been argued that the 1979 elections over which General Obasanjo presided were the only free elections held in the country between independence in 1960 and 1999. Obasanjo, a Yoruba man, presided over the elections which brought into power the Hausa dignitary, Shehu Shagari. Many fellow Yoruba continued to blame Obasanjo for not playing the ethnic card and handing over power to Chief Obafemi Awolowo.

The African renaissance should encourage heads of state to follow Obasanjo's example in his first administration in the 1970s and to bow out gracefully without unfairly playing the ethnic card. Obasanjo bowed out after less than four years. Leopold Senghor in Senegal bowed out gracefully soon after, but after 20 years in power. Normally heads of state should bow out after 10 years, and only in exceptional circumstances after 15 years. Obasanjo's second administration from 1999 should emulate the spirit of his first regime a quarter of a century earlier.

The African renaissance should strengthen the links between the academy and the media as two systems of information and knowledge. We might call this concept ACA-MEDIA (as distinct from ACADEMIA) linking the world of scholars with the world of reporters and journalists. The new South Africa may be moving in that direction. The links between scholarship and other modes of information and communication are bound to deepen. The African renaissance needs to respond constructively to the merging ACA-MEDIA, alongside the more traditional respect for ACADEMIA. The African renaissance should always pursue South-South co-operation, and pay special attention to Africa's friends in India, Malaysia, Pakistan, China, and of course Africa's more immediate neighbours in the Arab world, and in many other countries elsewhere.

WHAT IS AFRENAISSANCE?

In 1994 I was invited to a conference at the Central State University in Wilberforce, Ohio. There was one major condition imposed on the presenters of papers for this conference: no papers which were pessimistic about the African condition would be admitted. This was a conference for Afro-optimists, not for Afro-pessimists. I accepted the condition. I wrote a paper entitled 'Afrenaissance' (one word). If I had known that the term 'African Renaissance' was going to be so popular in southern Africa a few years later, I would have insisted on the immediate publication of my paper.

Unfortunately I gave the English language rights of my paper to the Central State University who have been in negotiations with Stanford University Press about publishing the whole proceedings. They are taking their time. To date the main published proof that I had written such a paper is in German. A German publication, *International Politik,* translated my paper and published it in 1996 in Volume 51, No. 9, 1996.

The Renaissance in the history of Europe was a return to the Greco-Roman classics. The European Renaissance was partly a liberation from the heavy hand of Christianity (imported from the Middle East) and an attempt to recover the spontaneity of ancient Greece at its best. Afrenaissance or the renaissance in Africa must also be in part a return to the classics. And what is a return to the African classics? It must involve a partial return to African culture and civilisation. The African renaissance must in part involve the re-Africanisation of Africa based on seven principles.

THE SEVEN PRINCIPLES OF AFRENAISSANCE

1. A new systematic recognition of the probable authenticity of African oral history (The history imperative)
2. A new respect for African languages and oral literatures (The language imperative)
3. A readiness to train, encourage and use African talent in all fields of human endeavour, from forestry to medicine, from business to nuclear physics (The talent imperative)
4. A recognition of Africanity as one of the dignified face of humanity (The dignity imperative)
5. A sustained capacity for self-reliance and self-development among African peoples (The imperative of self-reliance)
6. A reactivated will for humane self-rule and clean governance in spite of massive pressures to the contrary (the imperative of humane self-rule). Even soldiers like Gowon and Obasanjo could contribute to that spirit, let alone more saintly figures like Nelson Mandela and Archbishop Tutu.
7. A creative African response to a world of globalisation and historic trends (the imperative of creative accommodation to globalisation). Africa may have to teach the world the culture of a short memory of hate and speedy reconciliation.

The third principle of encouraging talent at all ages becomes important in its wider consequences in the arts and sciences, in literature and philosophy, and in practical skills. In 1998, the Modern Library Board of the United States issued its list of the 100 best novels published in the twentieth century in the English language. Was this a kind of linguistic apartheid based on English? The Modern Library Board (Random House) also ranked these novels. *Ulysses* by James Joyce was ranked first and foremost. And *The Magnificent Ambersons* by Booth Tarkington was ranked No. 100. The majority of the books were from the Commonwealth and almost all the rest from the United States.

No African novel in the English language made the first 100 – not even Chinua Achebe's work or the work of Nobel Laureates Wole Soyinka and Nadine Gordimer. Was this linguistic apartheid combined with racial apartheid? Not quite. While Africa was completely out of the league, the African diaspora did make it. Ralph Ellison's *Invisible Man* made it for No. 19, Richard Wright's *Native son* made it as No. 20 and James Baldwin's *Go tell it on the mountain* made it for No. 39. Muslims were relieved that the list did not include Salman Rushdie's *Satanic verses*, but the list did include Salman Rushdie's *Midnights' children* (No. 90). Books about Africa by non-Africans which made the list included Joseph Conrad's *Heart of darkness* (No. 67) and V.S. Naipaul's *A bend in the river* (No. 83), both of which also feature in Commonwealth literature.

Should we be alarmed that none of the great African writers made the list of the top 100? It would have been nice if Chinua Achebe's novel *Things fall apart* (1958) had been included in the list of the 100 top novels of the twentieth century. It certainly deserved to be. Other Achebe enthusiasts might vote for *Arrow of God* (1964) as Achebe's most profound novel. But none of his works made the list. Was linguistic apartheid verging on the racial?

There is a consolation. The only authors who made the list of the top 100 of the century whose mother tongue was not English were Joseph Conrad, Vladimir Nabokov and Salman Rushdie. All the rest were native products of Anglo-Saxon linguistic culture in one way or another. This includes V.S. Naipaul. They were native speakers of English. This means one of two things: either writing in English when English is not one's native language is a far greater handicap than we all assumed or the judges of the top 100 novels of the twentieth century were simply too Anglo-Saxon themselves. On balance I prefer the latter explanation. The judges were probably too Anglo-Saxon in their prejudices, even if some judges were from the Commonwealth.

As part of the African renaissance, it would be appropriate if by the year 2000, firstly, the ten best African novels of the twentieth century in any language, indigenous or European, were announced at the Zimbabwe International Book Fair or at the Indaba in Harare. Secondly, the ten best major poems in any indigenous African language could be publicized, and thirdly, there should also be a selection of the ten best plays in any European or indigenous African language. Finally, the ten best books for or by children from Africa in any language could also be selected:

> When the **little** heart we magnify
> And the sure vision celebrate
> And worship **mini-greatness** passing by
> Ourselves are great.

One may ask whether in a hundred years we should select a hundred works under each category rather than ten of each. There is a certain neatness in the Swahili concept of *mia kwa mia* ('a hundred by hundred'). A competition for the ten best novels in a hundred years would of course be ten times more severe than a competition for a hundred novels in a hundred years, but in either case Africa would be celebrating a convergence of high hearts, a constellation of sure visions. This would be the aesthetic side of the African renaissance. To paraphrase inversely another poet:

> Deign on the passing genius to turn thine eyes,
> And lean awhile on art to be wise.

If *francophonie* started as linguistic apartheid based on the French language, the Modern Library Board of the United States has drifted towards a form of linguistic apartheid based on the English language. The African renaissance aspires to transcend the apartheid of language, as well as of race. Ultimately the renaissance celebrates the high heart not in individual heroes but in the African continent, as a whole; it magnifies the sure vision not from citizen to citizen, but in the mighty will of the African people.

Chapter Nine

THE WAR IN AFRICA: A CHALLENGE FOR PARIS AND PRETORIA

Jean-François Bayart

The dismantling of the apartheid regime has led neither to the constitution of a strong political axis, nor to the development of a common approach to regional development between Paris and Pretoria – a double convergence that some wish for ... and others fear. The failure of this grand design – that while it remains to be realised must not hide the real improvement of relations between the two countries – has several causes. More competent observers than I will be in a better position to analyse them. The problem has anyway been decentred taking into account the international financial crisis and especially the extension of the conflicts south of the Sahara. It is henceforth in the face of the spectre of war that Paris and Pretoria must envision concerted responses. We must still come to a clear understanding of what causes war in Africa and what its real stakes are. That will be the aim of this chapter.

A POINTER: THE MUTINY OF THE ARMY IN GUINEA-BISSAU (JUNE 1998)

While Congo-Kinshasa has been in a new state of disruption and while the whole of Central Africa has been engulfed in it, and the Republic of South Africa, the only real industrial and democratic country of the subcontinent, is searching for its place in the regional equilibrium with difficulty while preparing for the succession of Nelson Mandela, it could seem curious to first fix one's attention on the conflict that is tearing apart little Guinea-Bissau, a particularly disadvantaged state with a population of one million. This new crisis, not the first of its kind in Africa, symbolises by itself the developments which are quietly at work in the sub-Saharan political societies.

Let us recall the facts succinctly. In January 1998 an arms trade benefiting the Senegalese rebels of Casamance was dismantled following an important discovery of arms at a road check at Bissau's exit. The army's General Chief of Staff, Ansumane Mane, was compromised and discharged. The day before the examination of his case by parliament and the judiciary at the beginning of June he took the initiative and launched a mutiny. Fearing the establishment of a new regime favourable towards the Casamanese rebellion at Bissau, Senegal intervened militarily at the request of President Vieira. Guinea also sent a small contingent. But the mutineers held the loyalist and foreign troops to a failure. It soon transpired that General Mane was benefiting from the support of the majority of an army hardened by the national liberation struggle against Portugal and who had a good knowledge of the terrain. The authorities suspected the Casamanese rebels as well as the Portuguese and Angolan mediators to have given him a strong hand. Solicited to re-establish the peace, the Community of the Countries of the Portuguese Language (CCPL) and then the Economic Community of West African States (ECOWAS) became divided and soon proved impotent. The snare of the war seemed to be closing in on Guinea-Bissau and Senegal whose army, already compromised in a ferocious repression of the Casamanese rebellion, was now stuck in the quagmire of its southern neighbour. Finally the CCPL obtained a ceasefire agreement on July 27 1998 and an accord on August 26 1998 without anybody being able to predict what the compromise between the protagonists would hold.

One finds in these somewhat incredible events and the stakes involved most of the elements that shape the destiny of sub-Saharan states. Above everything else there is the war. Led by a group of young officers that seems to have been the real instigators of Mane's uprising under the pretext of defending the claims of the 'old fighters' of the national liberation struggle, the mutineers were probably in a position the day before the ceasefire to offer a substantial resistance and to engender a growing regionalisation of the conflict which would have caused a flood of refugees (250 000 people had fled their villages with several thousand among them having reached foreign countries). From this point of view all danger has not been dispelled. By all accounts, in the coming months Senegal would remain at fault and would seek to distract attention from its domestic problems by trying hard to find the impossible military solution to the decade-old problem beyond its border in Casamance at the peril of its democratic soul. It is very improbable that the buffer zone envisioned by the accord of August 26 is more effective than the steps taken together during the last couple of years by Bissau and Dakar. Already engaged in the Sierra Leonian and Liberian crises, and present in Guinea and Gambia, Nigeria could be called upon at any moment by President Vieira, who appealed in vain for an intervention by the Angolan army in the second half of June. Nigeria could be tempted simultaneously to pursue an ambiguous game with dissidence: the conflict virtually supplies it with a new opportunity to weigh on its great francophone rival, the West African Economic and Monetary Union (WAEMU), which Guinea-Bissau had joined in 1997. Libya, which has made a spectacular comeback in Chad, and without doubt still remembers the arms deliveries which it carried out in Casamance at the beginning of the nineties with the help of Guinea-Bissau's army and General Mane, did not in its turn miss the chance to profit from the occasion. Furthermore, Mauritania and Gambia, which also lent their support to the manoeuvre to weaken Senegal, are likely to commit the same offence again.

Gradually the influential extra-African powers in the region will see themselves, if not sucked in, at least bothered by the troubles of Guinea-Bissau if the fighting breaks out again. Already President Vieira has denounced the support that Lisbon would have given to the mutineers and Paris has been accused by the Portuguese, Mozambican and Brazilian press of wanting disrupt Lusophonia through the intermediary of Senegal. Portugal and France, whose ministers of foreign affairs have agreed to act together and not allow this issue to strain their relations, were unable to avoid serious misunderstandings during the course of the summer. More fundamentally, the French government, which saw in Guinea-Bissau's adhesion to the franc zone the cornerstone of the currencies eventual spread to Guinea and Ghana, today participates in the political destabilisation of the WAEMU, just as the Central African Economic and Monetary Community (CAEMC) is prey to the upheavals in Congo-Brazzaville, the Central African Republic and Chad. This occurs at a stage when the delicate question of the relations between the CFA franc and the euro has not been settled: if the Council of European Ministers of Finance and Economy gives its 'political accord' on July 6 to the maintenance of the link between the two currencies, the precise modalities of this approval in principle still has to be defined between now and the first of January 1999 in a context where the reluctance of Germany and the European Central Bank is very real.

Certainly the ceasefire of July 27 and the accord of August 26 seem to have stemmed from the internal regionalising mechanism of the conflict of Guinea-Bissau. However, one wonders how long this will last? None of the basic political problems has been resolved. Numerous precedents do unfortunately give reason to doubt that the crisis is definitively resolved. In particular one cannot exclude the fact that General Mane's mutiny ended by giving birth to one of those headless, protean and fissiparous guerrillas forces which are ravaging several West African countries, starting with Liberia and Sierra Leone, and with whom it is very difficult to negotiate peace owing to the lack of representative leaders. From this point of view the Casamanese example is worrying: despite a multiplicity of mediators, President Abdou Diouf has never achieved constructive dialogue with the partisans.

Nevertheless, the elusive character of such conflicts must not conceal the tangible social stakes which they carry and which fuel them over the years. They often permit the male youth to affirm themselves on the political stage and to gain access to the resources of the modern economy, often by way of pillaging or predatory violence and the armed control of the most lucrative commercial flows as the wars of Chad, Somalia, Liberia or Sierra Leone have illustrated. These conflicts can lead to the hoarding of land by non-indigenous entrepreneurs as in Casamance or of the organisation of relations between shepherds and farmers as in Mali, Niger or Chad. They also illustrate historical cleavages that constitute social inequality and form the base of contemporary states.

In this respect the crisis in Guinea-Bissau is a model. It allows the old tension between the people of mixed race origin (coloureds) and the 'indigenous people' re-emerge. The former had been the principal collaborators of the Portuguese coloniser for whom they became its 'compradores' and administrative auxiliaries. They were in fact often natives from the Cape Verde Islands which at that time lived in close association with Guinea-Bissau. Then the coloureds gave their best cadres to the nationalist movement, the PAIGC, in particular to its charismatic leader, Amilcar Cabral, who was assassinated by the Portuguese PIDE in Conakry in 1973 with the probable complicity of President Sekou Touré. On the other hand, the majority of the PAIGC's fighters had been recruited from the 'indigenous' peasants, notably the Balante. After independence in 1975 the guardianship of the Cape Verdian coloured elite quickly proved to be unwieldy: in 1980 President Luis Cabral, Amilcar's brother, who had succeeded him as the head of the PAIGC, was overthrown and Guinea-Bissau broke its political links with the Cape Verde Islands. At first the new president, Bernardo Vieira of Pepelese origin, relied on the 'indigenous people'. Nevertheless, from 1986 he turned more obviously towards the coastal coloured elite who had been the great beneficiaries, with the Pepelese cadres, of the steps towards economic liberalisation, the latest nominations in the military hierarchy and the renewal of the leading positions of authority of the PAIGC. General Mane's mutiny gave vent to the frustration of the Balantes at this development.

At this level the conflict echoes the tensions between the coastal elite and the hinterland groups which one observes in most African-Atlantic states. In Senegal the cleavage was overcome politically in the fifties through the electoral victory of Léopold Sedar Senghor. In other countries – for example the Ivory Coast or Cameroon – it has lost its acuity for demographic reasons or because of the hegemony of real national political alliances. However, it remains an important factor in the struggle for power and the control of wealth in states like Gabon, Benin, Togo, Liberia, Sierra Leone and Guinea, where in the last three cases the cleavage between the Mandingese economic networks and those of the other groups is even greater. Above all the Angolan civil war finds its origin in an antagonism similar to that which is currently tearing Guinea-Bissau apart: the MPLA primarily represents the important coloured and 'assimilated' families of Luanda and Unita represents the interests of the black African elite of the interior in line with a distinct polarisation, the racial dimensions of which one could never underline sufficiently, and which is anchored in the trauma of several centuries of slave trade.

The interlocking of autochtonous socio-economic stakes and external interferences which characterise the crisis of Guinea-Bissau is thus typical of the realities of war in the whole of Africa. It is also thus that regional structures of conflict are constituted, likely to reproduce themselves during decades to come as modes of political and economic regulation. There is a 'stability of war', if one could say that, in the Horn of Africa, Chad, Angola, in the Great Lakes region or in the bloody binomial that Liberia and

Sierra Leone currently attest to: these are the real regimes that organise the change of power, the access to riches, the political mobilisation of the youth, the legitimisation of the authorities, the social change in the relations between the sexes or the ages, technological modernisation, monetarisation, participation in the world economy, the diffusion of the cultural modes of the great global village and their reinvention by the local players.

However, there is another aspect in which the crisis of Guinea-Bissau epitomises the development of the subcontinent. The arms trade in favour of the Casamanese rebels, the disclosure of which provoked the outbreak of General Mane's mutiny, in reality goes back to the beginning of the nineties as we have seen. It is public knowledge that the whole of the politico-military establishment of the PAIGC took part in it, including the entourage of President Vieira, not to speak of Vieira himself. And the simple lure of profit is sufficient to explain any motivation, better in any case than the pretended fighting or ethnic solidarity between the Balante of Guinea-Bissau's army and the Diolla dissidents of Casamance. To come to grips with the extent of the profit phenomenon one must recall that the spouse of one of the highest Senegalese leaders herself sold arms to the latter, that Senegalese officers participated in illegal precious wood trade on the border with Guinea-Bissau, that their adversaries did not for their part sneeze at drug trafficking, that the nomination by President Diouf of a string of 'Mr Fix-its' has made peace negotiations a real income that nobody wants to see disappear too quickly and that the strong man of the Socialist Party and Minister of Presidential Affairs, Ousmane Tanor Dieng, has carved out a solid reputation of wheeling and dealing for himself in the deleterious climate created by the laundering of dirty money by the formal economy. In short, under its guise of the wise child of democracy, francophonia and public development aid, Senegal is taking a very direct part in the 'criminalisation of the state' in Africa.

The legitimate holders of power are devoting themselves more and more to economic activities considered to be illegitimate by their own laws and by international morality or law. Thus in July the presidencies of the Republic of Niger and Chad were implicated in the trafficking of false Bahreini money, all the secrets, of which have not yet been unveiled, taking into account the lack of eagerness of the Ndjamena authorities to respond to the questions of the government of Manama. In the same vein, Laurent-Désiré Kabila did not shy away from naming Célestin Lamaghy, a man pursued for fraud and money forgery by the French and Belgian judiciaries, as Guard of the Seal.¹ At worst certain civil wars, for example those of Liberia or Sierra Leone, resemble the settling of accounts between rival bands wanting to take hold of the riches of the country. This permanent and, one could say, organic overlap between the spirit of lucre and the conduct of public affairs, which the events of Guinea-Bissau's crisis confirm, is henceforth inscribed in the heart of the African state. It does not signify a radical mutation of the latter, but rather a simple exacerbation of the 'politics of the belly' which has established itself as the privileged mode of government since the thirties in continuity with the previous regimes of domination and accumulation.² The relative novelty of the phenomenon is in its acceleration, to the resources which it is drawing from globalisation and the liberalisation of the world economy and its growing coupling with war. The question is how one should interpret it with respect to what is becoming of the state.

THE SUDDEN REVIVAL OF THE CONGOLESE CRISIS (AUGUST-SEPTEMBER 1998)

The crisis of Laurent-Désiré Kabila's regime brought to power in Kinshasa by a heterogeneous coalition in May 1997 was predictable. It soon became apparent that the overthrow of Marshal Mobutu did not enable the settlement of any of the problems that the latter had left to deteriorate, or that he had carefully kindled to divide his opposition and keep himself at the head of the state despite the erosion of the economy, the mobilisation for democracy and the pressures of his foreign backers. On the one hand, the steps of economic recovery were delayed – except for the vigorous start to a potentially promising monetary reform on June 30 199? – and the new system proved to be just as authoritarian, policed and corrupt as that of the defunct dictator. On the other hand, the foreign backers of the rebellion of October 1996 simply did not see their hopes fulfilled. Agrarian violence followed in Kivu and the Mai-Mai militias, composed of youngsters from the authochtonous ethnic groups of the region which sided in the rebellion with the Banyamulenge of Rwandan origin, turned against the latter from the end of 1997 to defend the commercial and land interests of certain local elites or plain escheat. Dispersed by the offensive of Kigali's forces in the tragic conditions of which we know, the ex-Rwandan armed forces and their *Interahamwe* militias did not waste time in regrouping and taking the conflict up again on the same

Rwandan territory. Uganda which also supported the rebellion of 1996 to dismantle the strongholds from which different armed movements benefiting from Sudan's aid and Zaire's indulgence (or powerlessness) operated, nevertheless had to contend with an unprecedented rise in strength of the Allied Democratic Forces (ADF), which swathed the south-western districts in fire and blood. As for the United States, it could not hide its embarrassment with the man they preferred to their old client, Marshal Mobutu, even if it tried to soften the ardour of the United Nations investigators charged with shedding light on the conditions in which tens of thousands of Rwandan Hutu had been massacred during the events of 1996–97. At the beginning of the year it was clear that Laurent-Désiré Kabila was not up to responding to the missions which had been assigned to him by those who had armed him and even fought for him most often. The refusal of the Ugandan and Rwandan presidents to participate in two regional summits organised in Kinshasa in May and June made the discord of yesterday's allies public.

Undoubtedly aware of his deception, Laurent-Désiré Kabila changed his strategy. No longer content with excessively favouring the second biggest component of the alliance which carried him to power – the armed movement of the 'Katangese gendarmes', actually the descendants of the soldiers of Moïse Tshombé that lived in exile in Angloa and fought against Unita for the MPLA, and more broadly the elite of Shaba of which he himself is a native – the chief of the Congolese state spoke out against the predations of the Ugandans in the east of his country, made overtures to Congo-Brazzaville, the Central African Republic and Chad, and tried hard to renew dialogue with the Kinese political class which he strongly and carelessly marginalised and dismissed, his Tutsi military 'councillors' – Rwandan as well as Banyamulenge – at the end of July. A few days later a new rebellion broke out – to be honest so quickly that one cannot help but think that it was planned and that the changes to the leadership of the Congolese army simply anticipated an imminent *coup d'état*. The rest is known: the rebels' arrival at Kinshasa's doors thanks to an audacious airborne operation provoked a regionalisation of the conflict with Namibia, Angola, Zimbabwe, Sudan and Chad siding with Laurent-Désiré Kabila to counterbalance the Ugandan-Rwandan intervention, while the Republic of South Africa tried in vain to mediate diplomatically.

For most of the observers the cause is clear: these events only confirm the decadence of the state south of the Sahara. In their eyes this regional evolution moreover concurs in particular forms with a more general trend that we observe in the whole of the world owing to the development of international relations of identity mobilisations, the rampant internationalisation of the economy and the triumph of market forces. There would have been much to say for this thesis which now hardly merits examination. The state is less in retreat than it is redeploying its modes of intervention.[3] It forms part of economic liberalisation. It is a key player of globalisation for which it does not cease to decree the norms, for example technical. In reality it is the idea of a neat border between the private and the public spheres which is problematical. Historians have long insisted on the interpenetration of the two categories which were at the base of the genesis of the absolutist, then of the representative state, and which we find again in the course of Colbertism in France and Whig liberalism in England. This ambivalence equally constitutes the 'politics of the belly' south of the Sahara.[4]

Under these conditions the exacerbation of the political conflicts in central Africa could also be interpreted, subject to inventory, as the painful manifestation of the process of the formation of the state, rather than the expression of its irremediable decline.

In the first place war contributes to the emergence of a 'system of states' on a regional scale as it did in Europe until halfway into the twentieth century. Political historians and sociologists have shown how the absolutist centralisation, then the bureaucratic rationalisation and the democratisation of the masses have largely proceeded from the antagonisms which, for example, England, France, Spain, Austria and Germany had opposed. It is certainly impossible to pretend that the same causes will produce similar effects in Africa – inasmuch as war was not a sufficient cause for the formation of the western state! But one cannot exclude it a priori.

The interventions of the different states of the region in the Congolese conflict give them precisely the occasion to develop their military capacities and to forge alliances according to their respective strategic and economic interests and their perfectly reasonable objectives. We have seen that Rwanda and Uganda's first concern is the establishment of a buffer zone on their western borders and that they do not refrain from profiting from the fabulous resources of the eastern Congo. Officially neutral, constrained to discretion by the sanctions against it, Burundi has nevertheless helped the rebels to seize Uvira: for Burundi it is also about setting up a security glacis, as well as staying in the game at Kivu to preserve its traditional position in the re-exporting 'hub' of agricultural and mining products of the rich province, a role which Rwanda is now disputing. Being the butt of the hostility of Uganda, which has militarily supported the autonomists of its southern provinces, Sudan has supported Laurent-Désiré Kabila from the moment that he split with Yoweri Museveni. Angola, already established militarily in Congo-Brazzaville and at Pointe-Noire thanks to the civil war between Pascal Lissouba and Denis Sassou Nguesso in 1997, and aiming to prevent Unita, which was driven from Kinshasa with Mobutu's fall, from re-establishing its read bases and to suppress the Cabindan autonomist movements, wanted to avert all risk of an alliance between its own dissidents and the Congolese rebellion by taking control of the mouth of the river: the fate of Laurent-Désiré Kabila, whom Angola reproached a few months ago for giving renewed facilities to Jonas Savimbi, is now in the hands of the authorities in Luanda. As for Zimbabwe, it could no longer dissociate itself from the fate of that province in which it has mining, industrial and strategic interests, besides the personal links between Laurent-Désiré Kabila and Robert Mugabe and the desire of the latter to establish himself in the face of South African power, not to mention his trying to re-establish his authority in his own country.

Naturally none of these policies, rational as they might be, is exempt from dangers or incoherencies. If it is militarily valuable for the MPLA to outmanoeuvre Unita, the goal of its eradication through armed conflict cannot be taken for granted and could even in this case be accompanied by an economic and financial disaster which already threatens to provoke the collapse of the international oil price and the increase of Angola's external debt. Suffering from a serious recession and numerous political scandals that have shaken the regime's stability, Zimbabwe could without doubt have done better than to launch into a military adventure. Uganda is seeing its reputation as the model child of foreign backers being tarnished – a reputation which meant so much in terms of foreign finance for it – and finds itself once again occupied by the agonies of civil war which President Yoweri Museveni prides himself on having halted, notwithstanding the evidence to the contrary, particularly in the northern districts. Finally the Rwandan Patriotic Front is for its part locking itself into a logic of terror and isolating itself more and more: from this point of view one should not overrate its standing with the Congolese Tutsis, who did not hide their disagreements with Kigali's leaders before the outbreak of the rebellion in August and increasingly feel that they are being purely and simply used by the very restrained group that has cornered the power and its resources thanks to the tragic victory of 1994.

Yet these contradictions or calculated errors, which do not in fact have anything particularly 'African' about them, do not by themselves betray a failing of the state. The reality of the latter and the force of nationalism south of the Sahara must not be underestimated. Since independence Africa has known only one real attempt at secession, that of Biafra, which failed.[5] The other civil wars that have cast a shadow over the subcontinent – for example in Angola, Mozambique, Chad, Liberia, Sierra Leone – have been about the control of central power and not about the unity of the state. We have even seen armed movements claiming the reconstitution of the state left behind by the coloniser as in Eritrea, Western Sahara or Somaliland. And inversely, the contemporary states whose borders coincide more or less with those of the pre-colonial states – for example Burundi and Rwanda – do not have fewer difficulties as one would expect! It is thus erroneous to think that all Africa's problems stem from the 'artificial' character of the borders that were imposed by the colonisers during the Berlin conference: these created political entities that are now older than a century so that the Africans have had time to get used to them, and is also what we see in the Muslim republics of central Asia after the fall of the Soviet Empire and what happened in Latin America after independence.

Therefore the Congo's unity is without doubt less threatened than the western powers want to believe. One could certainly not, in the long run, exclude the annexation or the 'satellisation', *de facto* or *de jure*, of certain of provinces by its neighbours. The state as a mode of political organisation is hardly dead, not in Europe and not in Latin America. On the contrary it is very unlikely that the provinces will secede in a sustainable fashion, even if the principle of federalism ratified by the National Conference seems to have been established. The political and especially the military weakness of the central power must not deceive us. The Congo evidently occupies the unenviable place of Germany during the seventeenth century and has become the playing field of regional ambitions. However, we can draw some comfort from the fact that the Congolese themselves, too busy surviving and trading, are fighting little among themselves, leaving this in the care of their turbulent neighbours while they wait for a kind of 'Westphalian' equilibrium to be negotiated. Perhaps they are also waiting for a viable project of national recovery to outline itself, to which Kabila, an anachronism of the sixties, has failed to shape.

In the second place, the Congolese national conscience is well and truly vigorous. It should plead in favour of the survival of the state, even if it is as an 'imagined community' – but is not that the essential if one believes the famous essay of Benedict Anderson?[6] The sequence of the two rebellions, those of 1996 and 1998, has thrown the sombre xenophobic capital that the national idea carries in full light. From the outset Laurent-Désiré Kabila was suspected of having entered Kinshasa with Rwanda's wagons. By evicting his foreign 'councillors' in July he certainly hoped to win the hearts of his compatriots, much like Mobutu had drawn handsome popularity from the disgrace of his Tutsian entourage at the beginning of the seventies. And in fact, if he has not as such convinced them of his competence and honesty, Kabila has at least succeeded in designating the enemy: the Tutsi, the fiend of external aggression, even if the latter is often an 'enemy on the inside' ... Thus the critical question of the citizenship of the Tutsi and Hutu populations of Rwandan, Burundian and Ugandan origins living on Congolese land sometimes for several centuries, or since the colonial era, finds itself posed again.

Herein resides one of the lessons of the current crisis. We see the rights of non-indigenous peoples progressively called into question south of the Sahara in the form of massive expulsions, pogroms or administrative and legal exclusions. That is how it is in Nigeria when the authorities brutally hunt millions of immigrants. Or in the Ivory Coast when President Konan Bédié tries to disqualify his principal opponent, the former prime minister Alassane Ouattara, by arguing against his Burkinese descent. Or also in Kenya, when President Arap Moi sparks off real ethnic purification operations in the Rift Valley to dislodge Kikuyu farmers and at the same time destabilise the democratisation process, in line with the 'strategy of tension' tested by Marshal Mobutu in Kivu or in Shaba. This problem of autochthony, which in a certain way nourishes nationalism in its most hideous dimension, reminds us that ethnic conscience is not the opposite of national conscience: it is in fact an ingredient of nationalism and it is often promoted by the public policies of the state itself. The danger thus resides rather in the development of racialising ethno-nationalisms in the service of the strong and militarised powers, that is to say in totalitarian powers, the genesis of which has been sheltered by the Great Lakes region has for several decades and which the Rwandan regimes successively led by Juvénal Habyarimana and Paul Kagame have sinisterly illustrated like two sides of the same coin. It is this kind of passion and ideology that Laurent-Désiré Kabila has tried to canalise in his favour by launching the hunt against the Tutsi in Kinshasa and by arming the Mai-Mai militias in Kivu, even to the point of favouring conditions for one of those senseless rebellions impossible to control and which would render the region absolutely ungovernable.[7]

Finally, in the third place, the unrest in central Africa makes it possible for the states which make up the region to recover a part of the national sovereignty which has been progressively eroded by their having been put under the tutelage of backers of international funds under the pretext of structural adjustment. The fall of Hutu power in Rwanda in 1994 and the overthrow of Marshal Mobutu in 1997 have shown the limits of French influence. Paris has widely drawn lessons from it by staying reserved in the face of the renewed outbreak of the Congolese crisis, but also by renouncing overt intervention in Congo-Brazzaville's civil war and by closing its bases in the Central African Republic. It is at the moment enough for France to hoard new permits in the Eldorado of oil that Angola reveals itself to be and hope for commercial spin-offs ...

But if 1997 symbolically consummated the defeat of France's traditional policy south of the Sahara, does not 1998 toll the bell for American patronage in the region? Obsessed by their will to punish the Sudan, the United States has diplomatically, financially and even militarily favoured the formation of a grand coalition directed against Khartoum. The Kampala-Kigali axe was but one of the constituent elements. In the Horn of Africa Eritrea-Ethiopia saw the task of supporting the allied Sudanese opposition militarily consigned to them. Bill Clinton's tour in April was supposed to give a particular lustre to the enterprise and to celebrate the Africa of the 'new leaders' as opposed to the Africa of the 'old dictators' pampered by France. We know what the outcome of that was. The principal power of the region, the Republic of South Africa, wanting nothing to do with the American initiatives with regard to the constitution of an African peacekeeping force, gave a cool reception to President Clinton's economic recommendations and made no secret of its convictions: Pretoria does not intend to abandon its very independent foreign policy and betray the historical allies of the African National Congress, even if it must call itself Ghaddafi or Castro. In the Congo the Kabila operation has turned into a fiasco. Ethiopia and Eritrea have entered into war. The Ugandan economic and political miracle has vanished. The United States finds itself compromised in the terror practised by the Rwandan Patriotic Front, much like France was trapped by the perpetration of the genocide of 1994. The terrorists who struck in Nairobi and Dar es Salaam are symbolic of how Africa is cruelly revealing the collapse of the Clinton administration's diplomacy. The latter has not understood that the 'new leaders' that they thought they could submit to their regional goals in fact had their own agenda.

A grandiose replica of the Somalian fiasco of 1993, the disaster of central Africa ordains the revenge of the political on the financial and economic conditionality of the multilateral institutions, the eternal problem of the 'maintenance of peace' and the interventions of the great powers. In a certainly chaotic fashion it propels the forceful return of the autochthonous state onto centre stage. However, the question is whether it will in a foreseeable future be able to impose a 'Westphalian peace' on a subcontinental scale, which is the only option that could allow for an economic upturn.

CONCLUSION

In the future it will definitely be a particular profile of the state which will affirm itself as a central player south of the Sahara thanks to the conflicts: it will be a predatory and militarised state, but also a 'trickster' state, skillfully drawing advantage from the interstices of the international economy and from the interface between the formal and informal activities, that is to say from the illegal activities of the latter. We see this state at work today in Angola, Uganda, Rwanda or Chad, Nigeria and, in a more marketable fashion in Mozambique, Benin, Gambia, Equatorial Guinea, the Comoros and the Seychelles. The good souls who are confusing the exercise of power and the primitive accumulation of power with 'good governance' will take fright at this. All those who know that the formation of the state in the West was a cruel combination of wars and crimes – to take up the vision of Charles Tilly again – will limit themselves to trying to understand better the social foundations, the political economy and the strategies of the 'trickster state'. It is supposed that one simultaneously studies its articulation in institutions and fluxes considered to be legitimate by the international system, as well as its systematic functioning on the scale of the continent.

In effect it is well and truly a 'system of states' that we must comprehend rather than a bundle of parallel national trajectories. The historic differentiation of the latter is undeniable as much on the level of social alliances as on that of 'political cultures'. Nevertheless, we cannot for example penetrate the mysteries of Mozambique's fabulous growth – 14 per cent according to the latest statistics! – if we leave licit and illicit relations with the South African economy or the strategies of Mauritius's manufacturers out of the account. In the same vein the fate of Gambia, Benin, Equatorial Guinea, Burundi, Djibouti, the Seychelles and the

Comoros are inseparable from their transactions with the large states (Senegal, Nigeria, Cameroon, Congo-Kinshasa, Ethiopia, the Republic of South Africa) or the regional communities (CAEMC, WAEMU, SADC) which they flank and parasitise. The inverse is moreover true, and the quite disembodied problematic of regional integration which the international backers encourage is in fact corroded by this invisible political economy. Most of the contemporary wars are the extreme expressions of the 'system of states' which has thus constituted itself south of the Sahara in as much as they carry a social and cultural dimension of terror that is without doubt implacable.

That is perhaps the most fruitful lesson that the analysis of African societies teaches us today. We should draw a better understanding of the ambivalence of other contemporary situations from it, particularly East European and Asian which do view the exercise of power, the extreme enrichment of their guardians or clients, the privatisation of the state, the affirmation of the ideologies of national or popular sovereignty, the practice of violence, the diversification of the economic spaces and functions and the reasoned bypassing of international norms in similar vein.

It remains to be seen whether Paris and Pretoria will in the coming years co-ordinate their regional policies in the face of this challenge.

---

1 *Le Monde*, 11 June 1997.
2 On this problem, cf. J.F. Bayart, *L'Etat en Afrique* (The State in Africa), Paris, Fayard, 1989 and (in collaboration with S. Ellis and B. Habou) *La criminalisation de l'Etat en Afrique* (The Criminalisation of the State in Africa, to be published by Indiana University Press in 1999), Brussels, Complexe, 1997.
3 Cf. the dossier 'La privatisation de l'Etat' (The Privatisation of the State) under the direction of Béatrice Hibou in *Critique Internationale*, 1 October 1998.
4 Cf. J.F. Bayart, *L'Etat en Afrique*, op. cit., and B. Hibou, *L'Afrique est-elle protectionniste?* (Is Africa Protectionist?), Paris, Karthala, 1996.
5 Katanga's attempt in 1960 was largely manipulated by foreign interests and moreover misfired by itself.
6 *Imagined Communities: Reflections on the Origin and Spread of Nationalism*, London, Verso, 1983.
7 On the problem of ethno-nationalism, cf. the dossier 'Crisis in Central Africa' in *Africa Today*, 45 (1), January–March 1988, in particular the article by Catherine Newbury, 'Ethnicity and the politics of history in Rwanda', pp 7–24.

GENERAL BIBLIOGRAPHY

Africa Institute of South Africa, Africa at a Glance, 1995/6. Pretoria: Africa Institute of South Africa, Pretoria, 1995

African National Congress, 'Foreign policy in the new South Africa: a discussion paper', Department of International Affairs, ANC, Johannesburg, October, 1993.

Alden, C. & J.P. Daloz, eds., *Paris, Pretoria and the African Continent: the International Relations of States and Societies in Transition*, Macmillan, Basingstoke, 1996.

Barber, J. & J. Barratt, *South Africa's foreign policy: the search for status and security 1945–1988.* Cambridge University Press, Cambridge.

Bayart, J.F., *L'Etat en Afrique*, Paris, Fayard, 1989.

——, S. Ellis & B. Hibou, *La criminilisation de l'Etat en Afrique*, Brussels, Complexe, 1997.

Bischoff, P-H. and Southall, R., 'The Early Foreign Policy of the Democratic South Africa', in Wright, S. (Ed) *African Foreign Policies*, Westview Press, Boulder, Colorado, 1999.

Bowman, L. 'The Subordinate State System of Southern Africa', *International Studies Quarterly*, 12, 3, 1968.

Carnoy, M., M. Castells, S. Cohen, & F. Cardoso, *The New Global Economy in the Information Age: Reflections on Our Changing World.* University Park, PA: The Pennsylvania State University Press, 1993.

Davies, R. & W. Martin, "Regional Prospects and Projects: What Futures for Southern Africa?" In Vieira, S.; Martin, W. & Wallerstein, I. (eds.) *How Fast the Wind? Southern Africa, 1975–2000,* Trenton, NJ: Africa World Press, Inc., 1992.

—— 'South African Regional Policy Before and After Cuito Cuanavale', in G Moss & I Obery, (eds), *South African Review 5,*: Ravan Press and Southern African Research Service, Johannesburg, 1989.

—— & D. O'Meara, 'Total Strategy in Southern Africa: An Analysis of South African Regional Policy since 1978', *Journal of Southern African Studies,* Volume 11(2) 1985.

Esterhuysen, P., ed., *South Africa in Subequatorial Africa: Economic Interaction.* Pretoria: Africa Institute of South Africa, Pretoria, 1994.

Gill, S., 'Globalisation, Market Civilisation and Disciplinary Neoliberalism', *Millennium*, 24, 3, 1995.

Gourevitch, P. 'Letter from the Congo: Continental Shift', *New Yorker*, 4 August 1997.

Grundy, K., *Confrontation and Accommodation in Southern Africa: The Limits of Interdependence.* Berkeley and Los Angeles: University of California Press, 1973.

——, *South Africa: Domestic Crisis and Global Challenge.* Westview Press, Boulder, Colorado. 1999.

Holden, M., *Economic Integration and Trade Liberalization in Southern Africa: Is There a Role for South Africa?* Washington, DC: The World Bank Discussion Paper No. 342, October, 1996.

Holland, M., 'South Africa, SADC, and the European Union: Matching Bilateral with Regional Policies', *The Journal of Modern African Studies*, 33, 2, 1995

Iheduru, O., 'Post-Apartheid South Africa and Its Neighbours: A Maritime Transport Perspective', *The Journal of Modern African Studies*, 34, 1, 1996.

Jaster, R. 'South Africa's Narrowing Security Options', in R Jaster, ed., *Southern Africa: Regional Security Problems and Prospects,* Gower, Aldershot, 1985.

Johnson, P. & D. Martin, *Apartheid Terrorism: the Destabilization Report*, The Commonwealth Secretariat in association with James Currey and Indiana University Press, London, 1989.

Krugman, P. & A. Venables, 'Globalization and the Inequality of Nations', *The Quarterly Journal of Economics*, 110, 4, 1995.
Legum, C. & Doro, M., eds., *Africa Contemporary Record 1988–89*. African Publishing House, New York and London, 1992.
Lewis, S. *The Economics of Apartheid*. New York: Council on Foreign Relations, 1990.
——,'Economic Realities and Prospects for Trade, Investment and Growth in Southern Africa', *Africa Insight*, 24, 4, 1994.
Mandela, N., 'South Africa's Future Foreign Policy', *Foreign Affairs*, November/December 1993.
Marshall, D., 'National Development and the Globalisation Discourse: Confronting 'Imperative' and 'Convergence'', *Third World Quarterly*, 17, 5, 1996.
McGowan, P., 'The Global Informational Economy and South Africa', in Carlsnaes, W. and Muller, M., eds., *Change and South African External Relations*. Halfway House: International Thomson Publishing Southern Africa, 1997.
Michailof, S., ed., *La France et l'Afrique: vade-mecum pour un nouveau vogage*, Karthala, Paris, 1993.
Molteno, R., 'South Africa's Forward Policy in Africa: Milestones on the Great North Road' *The Round Table*, 243, 1971.
Nkuhlu, M., 'South Africa's Trade Policy for the Region: Challenges and Strategies', *Global Dialogue*, June: 9–10, 1996.
Nolutshungu, S., *South Africa in Africa: A study of ideology and foreign policy*. Manchester: Manchester University Press, Manchester, 1975.
O'Meara, D., *Volks-kapitalisme: Class, Capital and Ideology in the Development of Afrikaner Nationalism 1934–1948*, Ravan Press, Johannesburg, 1983.
——, *Forty Lost Years: the Apartheid State and the Politics of the National Party, 1948–1994*, Ravan Press and Ohio University Press, Johannesburg and Athens, 1996.
Ottaway, M. *Africa's New Leaders: Democracy or State Reconstruction?*, Carnegie Endowment for Peace, Washington, DC, 1999.
Saasa, O., 'The South African Factor in the SADCC Transport and Communications Systems', in Van Nieuwkerk, A. and Van Staden, G., eds., *Southern Africa at the Crossroads*, Braamfontein, South African Institute of International Affairs, 1991.
Southall, R., 'South Africa' in T M Shaw, and O Aluko, eds., *The Political Economy African Foreign Policy*, Gower, Aldershot, 1984.
—— & G. Wood, *Control and Contestation: State Security in South Africa's Homelands*, A Report to the Truth and Reconciliation Committee, 1998.
Spence, J.E., *Republic Under Pressure: a Study of South African Foreign Policy*, Oxford University Press, London, 1965.
Smouts, M.C. *La France face au Sud: Le miroir brise*, Karthala, Paris, 1989.
Tsia, B., 'States and Markets in the Southern African Development Community (SADC): Beyond the Neo-Liberal Paradigm', *Journal of Southern African Studies*, 22, 1. 1996.
United Nations Development Programme, Human Development Report, 1996, New York, Oxford University Press, 1996.
Vieira, S.; Martin, W. & Wallerstein, I., *How Fast the Wind? Southern Africa, 1975–2000*, Trenton, NJ: Africa World Press, 1992.
Walker, E.A., *A History of Southern Africa*, Longman Publishers, London, 1962.
Wallerstein, I., *The Modern World-System II: Mercantilism and the Consolidation of the European World-Economy, 1600–1750*. New York: Academic Press, 1980.
Williams, R., 'From Huguenots to Humanism: Franco-South Africa Security Dialogue' *South African Journal of International Affairs*, 6:2, Winter, 1999.
World Bank, World Development Report 1996. New York: Oxford University Press, 1996.